www.ultimateweightloss.com.au

"I was 110 kgs, had tried every diet and hired personal trainer after personal trainer—but nothing worked. I would lose a little weight only to put it on again and more. It became a vicious cycle and I started to lose hope. Luckily I came across PRS Coaching for weight loss.

I have been seeing Natasa now for 3 months on a weekly basis and I have lost 10 kgs and dropped from a size 18-20 to a size 16. On my way to a 14!

For the first time I have confidence in my ability to maintain the weight loss as she has helped me change my way of thinking and motivated me to set goals and make them happen. I know nothing will stop me now.

I cannot recommend or speak highly enough of Natasa Denman. She has changed my life in just 3 months."

Jodie Dean—Operations Manager, Feb 2011

"I have been overweight most of my life. It started in my teenage years and since then I have been piling on weight every year. There have been many occasions where I have tried to lose it, you name it I have tried it—Jenny Craig, Weight Watchers, joining numerous gyms etc. Each and every time thinking that's it, this time I am doing it, only to revert back to my old ways a month later, feeling useless.

Until I started using the services of PRS Coaching. Natasa has a gift of showing you that change can be easy and you already have what it takes within you to achieve an optimal result. All you need is passion and you will succeed. She has not only helped me see great results already but has also given me the confidence I need to continue and not give up. After seeing her for only 5 weeks I feel there has been a fundamental change in my behaviour, I am more determined than I have ever been and I feel truly empowered.

I strongly recommend her services and encourage you to take that first step to a better life, whatever your goal is."

Marija Janev—Part Time Marketing Professional
and a Full Time Mum April 2010

"I always knew that I had to lose weight. I just lacked the motivation and knowledge on how to do it properly. Natasa showed me that it's not one big goal but lots of little goals. It really helped to put it into perspective and made the whole process seem less daunting. 9 weeks along and I have lost just under 10kgs but most of all I feel healthy and happy."

Katy Hocking—Aspiring Actress Nov 2010

"I started working with Natasa after leaving an unfulfilling course at university, feeling lost and lacking direction. Natasa introduced me to the world of SUCCESSFUL goal setting. Previously I had just a BIG list of all the things I wanted to accomplish—I would look at the list, get daunted and then never attempt anything. Through coaching she has shown me how to accomplish great things in such a short space of time.

I have since opened my own business, Grace Eadie Photographer and am also working on developing myself even further as a recording artist/vocalist by breaking down my limiting beliefs. I would hate to think where I would be without the invaluable life skills Natasa has taught me!"

Grace Eadie—Photographer and Recording Artist May 2011

"As a twenty-two year old girl without a career as such so far in my life, at first I questioned what benefit life coaching would actually give me. However, after spending two months with Natasa, my whole outlook on life has changed. The main things I focused on with Natasa were my university degree and what comes after that, my personal budget and my weight loss goals. Through my work with Natasa I have realized that all these things in life (career, success, health) are interlinked, and I need to strive to achieve all of my goals, no matter how unreachable they sometimes seem, so I can live a quality life. Despite focusing on just these above things, Natasa has also helped me develop more as a person and I have since created a whole new perspective on life. I spend far less time worrying about the 'little stuff'. I am now able to ignore the problems that used to affect me as I now understand that I am in power of my own emotions and feelings and can make the choice to not let them bother me. This has enabled me to become a better friend, partner and person, and has also helped me get my friends and family through difficult times. I know I will continue to refer to the tools I have learnt from Natasa all through my career, relationships and life!"

Lauren Kenrick—High School Teacher, June 2010

"After undertaking coaching with Natasa, I found my focus and business grow in such a short amount of time. She is so motivating and is outstanding at addressing areas that need attention. She was able to help me shift my focus to the things that matter and make a difference. I now find I use my time much more efficiently and have more time to do the things I enjoy."

Anna Kennedy—Chiropractor, Aug 2010

THE 7 ULTIMATE SECRETS TO WEIGHT LOSS

THE 7 ULTIMATE SECRETS TO WEIGHT LOSS

NATASA DENMAN

Copyright © 2011 Natasa Denman
Reprinted 2013

ISBN 978-0-9875-9975-9
Ebook 978-1-4568-9320-0

All rights reserved. No part of this book may be reproduced or transmitted in any form or by any means, electronic or mechanical, including photocopying, recording, or by any information storage and retrieval system, without permission in written form from the copyright owner.

This is a work of fiction. Names, characters, places and incidents are either a product of the author's imagination or are used fictitiously, and any resemblance to any actual persons, living or dead, events, or locales is entirely coincidental.

To order this book, contact the author
Natasa Denman at natasa@ultimateweightloss.com.au

Contents

The Purpose and Intention of This Book 1
My moment—Starting out 3
My Husband's Story 7

Part 1

Chapter 1: Ultimate Weight Loss Secret 1: Goal Setting 13
Chapter 2: Ultimate Weight Loss Secret 2: Get Organised! 23
Chapter 3: Ultimate Weight Loss Secret 3: The Four Levels of Critical
            Thinking and the Six Core Human Needs 35
Chapter 4: Ultimate Weight Loss Secret 4: Language 47
Chapter 5: Ultimate Weight Loss Secret 5: Diet 54
Chapter 6: Ultimate Weight Loss Secret 6: Exercise 60
Chapter 7: Ultimate Weight Loss Secret 7: Mindset 69

Part 2

Chapter 8: The Ultimate Secret to Outstanding Relationships 83
Chapter 9: The Ultimate Secret to Fantastic Finances 96
Chapter 10: The Ultimate Secret to Successful Parenting 111
Chapter 11: The Ultimate Secret to Business Success 122

Afterword 135

To all individuals willing to take 100% responsibility for their lives and drive their own bus to success and fulfilment.

To my family, my big 'Why', to be the best version of me so I can make a difference in our lives and pay it forward to thers on a global scale.

The 7 Ultimate Secrets to Weight Loss

It's so much easier to say, 'I can't' and believe it than to ask, 'How can I?' and follow through.

(Heather Swann, *No Ceiling*, May 2006)

The Purpose and Intention of This Book

Having read many self improvement books and philosophical explanations of human behaviour, I really wanted to make this book very practical and hands on for you, the reader. If you are anything like me, you want a step-by-step system that will assure success in your pursuit to lose your unwanted weight. The concepts, facts, and actions to take as set out in this book will guarantee you get to your goal weight in the fastest time possible.

Everything discussed and suggested in this book has been researched and proven to work. I have no doubt you will have amazing results by gaining the understanding and tools along the way.

This book is not just a weight loss book. It can be applied in many different areas of life where you may be stuck and want momentum to move forward. If you follow the principles and structures, then you will have the results. It is you that will make the changes and that means taking 100 per cent responsibility for your actions and outcomes going forward. Drive your own bus and live life on your terms now and forever!

My moment—Starting out

'Hurry Up,' someone called. It was the evening of my twenty-eighth birthday as my friends bustled through the doorway. It was the moment I stood in front of the mirror of my small one-bedroom apartment. I looked at myself, my clothes (a beautiful, formal, blue dress), make up . . . All done up. Something wasn't right! I wasn't happy with the woman who starred back at me.

She wasn't overweight, definitely not obese, but she was frumpy, un-toned, and unhealthy looking. That was my defining moment! I realised that I didn't have the body I used to have. There had been years spent establishing a career and leading a hectic lifestyle, years spent living alone and not cooking, years of late nights, alcohol, and food consumption with no concept of what's good and what's not so good—Nutrition hadn't been on my social calendar. I really had no idea even what a scale looked like or what I weighed. I just knew I didn't like what I saw in that mirror. Knowing what I know now, I was 10 kg from my ideal body image. My husband, then boyfriend, was also just about tipping the scale at around 100 kg. We had some work to do and some re-educating to accomplish before we would be at a healthy and good-looking weight.

Here was a new challenge. Something I never had to tackle before in my life. Where to start? Do I know anyone that has been successful at losing weight? I didn't believe in fad diets because in the long run they are not sustainable. I wasn't going to pay weight loss companies huge amounts of money to deliver food for me because that wasn't going to teach me anything. So a few weeks went by, and as we coaches like to say, 'What you focus on is what you get to the exclusion of everything else.'

It came to us out of nowhere! My mum had bought the book *CSIRO Total Wellbeing Diet* because a lot of her work colleagues were using it and were having great success.

We skimmed through the book. It was easy to read and included structured twelve weeks of menu plans that contained all the foods I would normally eat. All we had to master was the preparation and correct measurements of all the meals.

The first week, it took us literally two hours to organise our list and even more time to do the shopping. But we were determined and motivated to get started. It was tough in the first three to four days. We felt hungry all of the time, and the meal times couldn't come soon enough. After the first few days, the hunger pangs subsided and our bodies adjusted to the new portion sizes and types of foods we were eating—low carbohydrate and high protein foods.

Each week, the planning time got shorter and so did the shopping. We were becoming experts at the new diet and way of life. I couldn't believe my eyes as each week we saw the kilos drop off. I was losing around half a kilo and my boyfriend 1.5 to 2 kg per week. We did the programme for ten weeks before heading overseas and I managed to lose 5 kg and my boyfriend 15 kg. Although I believe exercise is a must as a perfect compliment to any diet, I will confess that we didn't do any during this period.

Diet is 80 per cent of the struggle won. Exercise will increase your success by toning you up and speeding up the weight loss. It will give you more energy and induce endorphins that will make you happy to keep moving towards your ideal goal weight. Nowadays, I like to be moving each and every day—if not during official exercise time, then, incidentally, I manage to raise my heart rate at least a few times per day.

That wasn't the end of my weight loss journey. My ideal body image was a particular female celebrity who is my height but weighs 6 kg less than my 60 kg. This was the weight I was after the use of the menu plans. The best thing the book created for us were new habits such as a healthy breakfast every day, knowing what's good for lunch, avoiding full sugar drinks, and keeping our portions small. We continued this throughout the next year, and when the CSIRO released their second book after the huge success the first one had, we were more than happy to do another round of the menu plans. There were lots of yummy new recipes to try out.

This is where my last 5 kg fell off and I reached my goal weight. I no longer had a flabby tummy, and I looked toned and fantastic in a bikini. You may be asking yourself how I did it and what motivated me and kept me going when I was tempted or hungry? I put it down to a couple of qualities I possess: my unbelievable stubbornness and the ability to follow instructions perfectly. There were times I was craving either sweet or salty foods, but I just had to distract myself or get a healthy snack to keep going.

The funny thing that happened when we were doing the programme *CSIRO Total Wellbeing Diet—Book 2* was that we realised that I had put my boyfriend on the female version of the diet the first time around. No wonder he dropped so much weight in such a short period of time. We had a good laugh! Having a buddy on your weight loss journey that will support you, eat the foods you are eating, and accompany you on the walks and exercise is a great bonus and makes the whole experience easier and more fun. Could I have done it without him or him without me—that I don't know . . .

My Husband's Story

There comes a time in everyone's life when they make a decision to try to change their current state. Some have a tragedy befall them like the loss of a loved one. Others might have a health scare such as a heart attack. Fortunately for me, it was neither of these events.

I had just got back from a golf weekend with some friends from high school that I hadn't seen for some years. I was rather embarrassed when I shared with my wife that I was the largest of the twelve people on the golf weekend. I was not the classic obese person that you would see on *The Biggest Loser* but for a twenty-eight-year-old man, I was certainly not in good shape.

I had become stuck in a comfortable place where alcohol and food were consumed in an unhealthy way. Most nights would consist of beer and takeaway food—an unhealthy combination as it was added to the fact that I smoked and rarely exercised. There was too much socialising going on and there was no self-control. All of these things I knew.

My then girlfriend, Natasa (the author of this book), my present wife, was also not happy with the way she was looking and feeling after her birthday. I'd like to say that 'we' decided to do something to change our situation, but it was Natasa's decision to try an alternative eating plan.

This soon became my nightmare. The 'Total Well-being Diet' commenced a day later. There was no time for procrastination—no time for backing out. Natasa is a woman of action, and once she committed to her plan, I was strapped in for the ride.

The preparation of the shopping and menus seemed to take forever. Admittedly, we had to start from scratch as we had no food in the house and hadn't had to Supermarket shop for several years. This got easier as the weeks went by, and very soon, we were preparation experts.

It was great food. It was never that I didn't want to cook. I am actually a novice chef who has great skills in the kitchen. I just hadn't practised these skills for years.

I was so hungry for the first few days. My stomach felt as though my throat had been cut! I wanted to cheat. I can admit that now, but I never did. On Day 3 of the diet, I bought a packet of chips on the way home, but thankfully, I threw them in a bin. I knew that Natasa was hungry too and knew that she would never give in to temptation. (She is just too stubborn!)

After I saw the weight start to fall off me almost immediately, I started to enjoy our new lifestyle. We talked about how this fresh food was making us feel great, and friends and family started to see the change in my physical appearance as well as my emotional state.

I lost fifteen kilograms in ten weeks. It did accelerate my weight loss as the one thing Natasa overlooked in the food quantity preparation was to take into account that, as a male, I should've been eating larger portions. I still think she did it on purpose, even though she swears innocence to this day.

I felt great when I saw the same friends three months later at a wedding. I was then the same size as my friends, and I was told that I looked five years younger than the rest of them. The sense of accomplishment I felt after making a plan and sticking to it was fantastic.

We now have a son and are able to be great role models for him as we talk about healthy and unhealthy foods with him as it is now all we know. If I had not committed to making a change in my life when I did, who knows how my life might have turned out?

Don't wait for a life-shattering event to force you to act. Commit to making the changes in your life that you so desperately want today! Not tomorrow.

All of the above was five years ago, and since then, we have maintained a healthy and well-balanced diet with plenty of exercise and support for one another. After having my first child two and a half years ago, my body bounced back to pre-baby shape in a matter of weeks. I am carrying our second child at the moment and have no doubt in my mind I will be my ideal body image after that as well.

Once you know what it takes to lose weight and keep it off—you just know! You can do it over and over again if you slip up. And slip-ups are part of life. No one is perfect!

The question is: How do you get yourself in that mindset and maintain it long-term? That's why I am here to share with you some simple tools, secrets, and strategies that will help you on your journey—not only will you lose weight, but you will attain skills in other areas that are transferable to other parts of your life. And you may save some money along the way . . .

Make a *decision* today that this is going to work. It is only when we decide this that we can move forward to making it a reality. A weight-loss journey takes time and patience (mine took close to two years, but I have never looked back). There isn't a shake, pill, or a quick-fad diet out there that will enable you to create the changes I will be sharing with you throughout this book. So buckle up and enjoy the ride. Most importantly, *take action*!

PART 1

CREATING YOUR ULTIMATE BODY

Chapter 1

Ultimate Weight Loss Secret 1: Goal Setting

> Look to the future, because that is where
> you'll spend the rest of your life.
> (George Burns)

Goal setting is a familiar subject for most people. Yet most do not practice it. In fact, 95 per cent of people do not set goals and fail, and 5 per cent of people that do, succeed. This is a figure taken from research and has been proven to be right time and time again. So why do people continue to go through life wandering aimlessly and without setting goals?

For this reason, the first chapter is the number one ultimate weight loss secret. Before you learn about nutrition and training, goal setting and mind dynamics are essential to ensure your success on this journey.

Goal setting is like any other habit. That's right. It needs to become a habit in order for your unconscious to start putting into place a successful permanent behaviour change in your diet and exercise. *Repetition* is an effective way to get your goals through to your unconscious mind because 95 per cent of our behaviour is unconscious and automatic. Wouldn't you want weight loss and weight maintenance to one day become something that happens on auto pilot?

Your will only change your body when you start creating new habitual patterns of thinking and visualising.

How Do You Know Where You Are Heading Without a Vision In Hand?

So 9.5 out of 10 people do not set goals! It's staggering how many of us rely on luck and just taking whatever life brings. I don't know about you, but I like having the power to plan and create my ideal life whether this is to do with work, relationships, health, material things, income, goals, contribution, or personal development. I love knowing what direction I am heading in and exactly how long it will take me to get there.

Goal setting is simple, easy, and lots of fun. You get to use your imagination and put down things you really would like to achieve going forward. By writing down your goals and reading them daily, you stay focussed and on track.

The Best Goals to Set Are 90-Day Goals!

Ninety days is usually long enough to work on a particular goal and short enough to keep you under some pressure and focused. When you learn how to set your goals properly, it will become an activity that is very enjoyable and quick to do.

Even when I didn't know how to set goals properly, I still wrote a number of wishes at the start of every new year in my new diary. These were things that I intended to work on over the next twelve months. I would be quite amazed to review them months later and realise that 80-90 per cent of what I wrote was accomplished and ticked off that list. Nowadays, I set my goals more regularly using the 'SMART' template that I will share later on.

It is the unconscious mind that gets the commands embedded when setting goals. The proof here is that I wouldn't remember what I had written in my diary back on 1 January each year, even a week after the fact. The sheer exercise of thinking what I wanted and putting it on paper was embedded into my unconscious at the time of writing. It was this that made me work on what I wanted to achieve and have in that year.

I read somewhere: 'Millionaires read their goals once a day, billionaires read them twice!' How many times will you read yours?

Imagine having the power in your hands to change your current reality and have a say in what will transpire in the near future. I am here to share the secret of goal setting and breaking them down into smaller chunks. This is important so that you can reward yourself when you reach a milestone. It will keep the motivation going and make you work harder to get to the next reward.

S.M.A.R.T.

The SMART template is the most widely used way of making sure your goals are set the right way. Each letter of the acronym stands for something different, and there has been a few different versions of what each letter stands for. Here is the one I like and use every time I set a goal.

'S' stands for *specific*—a specific goal has more chance of being accomplished than a general one. The more specific, the better. For example: I would like to be fitter. A more specific example of this would be: I plan to swim twice a week and go to the gym three times per week. To make this section of goal setting easier, you could ask yourself the following questions:

1. Who: Who is involved?
2. What: What do I want to accomplish?
3. Where: Identify a location.
4. When: Establish a time frame.
5. Which: Identify requirements and constraints.
6. Why: Specific reasons, purpose, or benefits of accomplishing the goal.

'M' stands for *measurable*—when you set measurable goals, you have the ability to know when you have achieved them and if it has been within the time frame set out. They keep you focused on the how much or how many. It also helps to ask yourself the question: 'How will I know when I have achieved my goals?'

'A' stands for *attainable*—setting goals that are important to you tend to start focusing on how you can make them come true. You start looking for alternatives on reaching a particular goal and you are more open to other opportunities that may not have been obvious to you earlier.

All goals are attainable if you break it down into smaller steps and work out a wise time frame that allows you to carry out those steps. They start appearing more within reach as you grow and expand to match them. You see yourself as worthy of these goals, and you start developing the attitude, traits, and personality that will allow you to possess them.

'R' stands for *realistic*—in this part of goal setting, you need to ask yourself: Do I really believe I can achieve this goal? Often, setting more difficult goals is better because you get to have more motivational drive in achieving them. In saying that, though, having a goal that is far out of reach may demotivate you since your belief in attaining it may not exist. It is great to stretch yourself and set your goals more frequently so that you get the feeling of being successful and you start building reference points for success. This will build your self-belief in achieving bigger future goals.

'T' stands for *timely* or *tangible*—the first thing I would start with in goal setting is this part. Having the date adds that sense of urgency to a goal, and it sets your unconscious mind into motion to begin working on that goal.

Finally, a goal is tangible when you can experience it with one of your senses. Those are touch, taste, smell, sight, or hearing. The three most common senses I would describe my goals in are to ask myself to describe: What am I going to hear, see, and feel when I achieve this goal? This makes the goal tangible, and it has a better chance of making it even more specific and measurable.

Now that we have the criteria for setting goals, I would like to take you through how you would go about writing out a goal and an example of a perfectly composed goal that you can model to write out all of yours.

There are a couple of very important things in addition to the above criteria that must be noted and remembered: *Always write your goals in the present tense and 'as if' you are already in possession of them!*

Example:
It is 25 June 2011, and I am standing on the scales in my bathroom seeing 95 kg. I have lost 10.5 kg in the past twelve weeks. I feel full of energy and start hearing my family and friends make comments about my appearance. I see that my clothes are looking looser and feel baggier. I can now fit into an old pair of jeans I have never got to wear from ten years ago. I am going to the gym four times per week and walking twice a week. My diet is well organised and full of fresh

"Whoever wants to reach a distant
goal must take small steps."

Helmut Schmidt

fruit, vegetables, protein, and grains. I plan my menu for the week and shop accordingly. I am looking forward to the next milestone, but today I am going to reward myself with a ninety-minute massage and pampering treatment.

(Refer to Appendix C section for a SMART Goal Setting Template you can use when setting your goals.)

As you can see, the above goal is very specific, measurable, attainable, and realistic. It has all the different senses described. It paints a picture of the day when it is achieved and exactly how the person knows they have got it.

Goals should be an organic document that can be amended and reset in order to be really congruent with what direction you make a decision to move in. That is why reading them regularly will allow you to review and edit them as needed.

Remember, the secret of the most successful people is that they set goals and align themselves towards achieving them. This should always be your first step in designing your ideal future and, in the case of this book, your ideal body image.

Warning: Always Break Down Your Goals into Bite-sized Chunks

If you have a goal to lose a lot of weight (for example, 50 kg), it is a great idea to break this goal down into 5 or 10 kg smaller goals. Setting a goal for the whole amount may seem overwhelming and demotivating. The smaller goals will seem more believable and within reach. Also, make sure that a reward is put in place when a milestone has been reached, each and every time, to keep your motivation up and drive you towards the next steps.

Share Your Goals

Letting loved ones know what your goals are will help and push you even harder towards achieving them. When you tell someone you are going to do something, it is in our human nature not to want to let them down. In coaching, we call this 'The Law of Consistency'. We like to stick to our word, and if we don't, it can make us look inconsistent and non-congruent with what we promised to achieve. Use the power of this law to push you towards action and focus on what you want to achieve.

Vision Boards

Another way of attracting what you want in your life is to have clear pictures of your wants and desires. If you can imagine it and have a picture of what you are wanting, that's a great way and a step closer to manifesting it in your life. The Law of Attraction is a powerful one, and this has been proven by many people. They all have these two things in common: goals and vision boards. So start yours today!

Vision boards are fun to do and allow you to dream up anything your heart desires. They are meant to include things that you may think at the moment are impossible. It's important to have dreams that are scary, because if you aim for the stars and only reach the moon, you have still achieved amazing results because your focus is on unbelievable success.

The best place to start is to brainstorm all the things you would like in your life going forward. Here are some questions and ideas of what you may want to put on your vision board:

1. The type of home you'd like to own
2. Holiday house/apartment and where
3. Destination you'd like to visit
4. Adventures you would like to have
5. An ideal body image picture of someone you admire that is similar to you
6. A business you may like to start and have or your ideal job
7. Particular shops you may want to shop in, for example, Chanel, Gucci, and so on
8. Your dream car or cars
9. Material things you would like to have (pictures of them)
10. If you want children, have pictures of babies with the sex you prefer on the board
11. You can have special quotes or numbers on your board, such as financial independence, success, stylist, nanny, and so on
12. Your big 'Why' you want all of the above

I trust this gives you a starting point in creating your vision board. Now go out there and get yourself a magnetic white board, markers, and tiny magnets to stick your pictures up with. This way, your vision board can alter and change as you do. It's the same as your goals. Review it and make amendments as time passes because your desires will change with your growth.

Easy and Fast Tip for Finding the Right Images for Your Vision Board

Once you have brainstormed up all the things that you want images of on your vision board, the easiest spot to find them is by 'googling' them on the Internet. What you need to do is enter exactly what you want in the Search field of Google and then press the Images word that appears on the top left-hand corner of your open page. This will bring up many images under that search that you can choose from.

Once you have found an image that you like, simply click on it so it comes up bigger and copy and paste it into the standard Paint programme that is found on all computers. From here, you can put a few images on one page. Once you have filled your page, print it off on a colour printer. Cut out your images separately, and start creating your vision board collage.

Going through magazines is the old laborious way of finding images for your vision board. With Google, you will have the exact image you are after in one-tenth of the time. Once you have brainstormed up all your images, the rest should only take you a couple of hours to complete.

A great spot to put your vision board is the office or dream space of your home. I also like to take a photo on my phone of my vision board and place it on the Home screen so that every time I refer to my phone, that is the first thing I see on it. I am always seeing exactly what I want, and my drive to get there is increased dramatically.

Cause and Effect (Which Side Are You Living On?)

Having goals means you are living at 'Cause' for what happens in your life. You know you are 100 per cent responsible for the results you achieve, and this makes you the captain of your ship. When living at Cause, you look for solutions to your problems and challenges, and you respond to frustrations in a positive and proactive way.

The 'Effect' side of the equation is weaker, non-desirable, and unproductive towards reaching goals. People living on this side tend to be into blaming others for the situation they are in. They have all the excuses and reasons as to why they are the way they are. Problems overwhelm them, and they tend to live reacting towards them. Living to the effect of the environment and those around you is much harder and more stressful.

Not everything we do in life is going to be fun and comfortable. Stretching ourselves is the only way to grow and experience new things, situations, and people. Living inside our comfort zone limits us physically and mentally to move beyond our current situation and create a life that is satisfying and fulfilling. Everyone aims ultimately for *happiness*, yet the mark is often missed because they listen to that little voice in their head called our *ego* that was designed to protect us from danger in distant, ancient history.

Have the curiosity to learn and grow like a child has it when it is seeing new things for the first time. Be willing to make mistakes and stuff it up because, after all, in life, *There is no* failure, *only* feedback*!* You will only learn how not to do it next time and exactly what your new options are. As the famous saying goes: 'It's better to have tried and failed than not to have tried at all.'

You decide your destiny, you decide who to love, befriend, and have as your mentor. Start this journey with your goals in hand, and you will soon realise it is not the destination, but the journey you live through that makes your life perfect for you. Always remember you are at the exact right position right now that you need to be—the rest is up to you.

What Is Your Purpose in Life—Your Big *Why*?

It's a very deep question, but have a good think about it. What were you put on this planet to achieve? Everyone has a purpose, and your journey to greater self-awareness is to get to know yours. Is it to help others, raise a family, work for a charity, or educate and mentor in your expertise?

My purpose is to reach out to as many people as I can globally and touch their hearts and minds with motivation and tips to help reduce this obesity epidemic the Western world is going through. I want to be their mentor and teacher so that they know what to do to regain control over their health and bodies. I understand that it is often education that is missing from these households, and I am here to change it and make and impact on a grand scale.

Top 3 Tasks to Be Completed from This Chapter:

1. Set your ninety day and one year goals using the SMART template.
2. Read your goals daily and share them with your nearest and dearest.
3. Put together your own Vision Board.

Chapter 2

Ultimate Weight Loss Secret 2: Get Organised!

*Out of clutter, find simplicity. From discord, find harmony.
In the middle of difficulty lies opportunity.*
(Albert Einstein)

Another habit for you to see successful weight loss and sustainable results is to organise and prioritise the things in your life. Not only will this ensure you shed your unwanted weight, but it will improve many other areas where you may be feeling rushed for time. Being organised assures that you will take the actions towards the goals you set in the previous chapter.

After setting your goals, it's important to take the time and break them down into an action plan. We are all busy but have the same twenty-four hours per day. Just think about Donald Trump and Bill Gates. These two individuals run hundreds of companies at the same time and still manage to have time for fun, family, and work. It's possible, and we all have control over how much we do and what we prioritise to keep ourselves busy.

Buy a Diary and *Use It Every Single Day*!

It is amazing the amount of people that do not own one even for important events or appointments. Relying on you to remember what needs to be done when all we seem to hear is how busy people are is a poor way of managing your life. If I can teach you anything at all, this is my favourite section of the book to enable you to run your life effortlessly. You will achieve so much more having direction and a plan of how each day will play out.

Why Use a *Diary*?

A planner or diary gives you a quick snapshot of what needs to be done on a particular day. You could choose to write in what you eat (as a weight-loss journal), your thoughts, appointments, and tasks that need completing. The uses are many and varied. My suggestion would be to decide what you consider to be your weakness and use it for that. Doing things that come easy for you won't implant any new habits in how you plan your days.

I understand some people like spontaneity and things to occur in an unplanned way. And that's OK. Schedule in a couple of days per week you don't plan anything at all—leave it to chance and do what you feel like as a reward for completing and sticking to your tasks at all other times.

No one lost any weight being totally disorganised. It takes time to plan your week's meals and shop for them. It takes planning to schedule in time for exercise, family, work, and your home. One of the biggest complaints I have from my clients is the lack of time they seem to have—yet when I ask them to perform a time audit for one or two weeks of their normal everyday life, we find many opportunities have been wasted either by oversleeping, watching TV, too much socialising, or just simple procrastination. To perform a time audit for yourself, you can use the template in Appendix B.

What Kind of *Diary* Should I Use?

My favourite type of diary is something in an A4 size that has a week per view. You can plan your time for the days by filling in the columns. I like this type because it gives you a quick snapshot of what your week looks like and enables you to space tasks and appointments easily, without overbooking one day and under-booking others.

For those of you that might use a diary for a number of things that won't fit in one column, I would get a day-per-page A4 size diary. This type will give you lots of space to write your thoughts in, enter the food you have eaten, and enter any tasks and appointments booked for the day. The disadvantage is that you cannot look at your week in one go, and it seems that all the weeks tend to blend into one another.

Really small diaries are only good for tasks and appointments and can be carried around in a handbag easily. I actually chose to buy a handbag that would fit my A4 diary rather than the other way around.

Whatever you choose, ultimately it's better to have one than not to have one at all. Get into the habit of using it daily. Remember: *It takes twenty-one days to create a new* habit! Test this notion and see what happens. You may be surprised how easy it is. And you will start noticing that you are calmer, in control, and getting more done than ever before.

How Exactly Do I Use a *Diary*?

Firstly, you must have your goals in front of you. Break them down into action steps that need to be taken so they can be achieved within the time frame specified. Enter any mini milestones into your diary that will keep you on track and allow you to monitor progress more frequently (once a week is the best).

Before you start planning your week, it is good to coordinate your schedule with that of your partner and kids' activities. This way you will avoid any clashes and slot in everything else around that.

Each Sunday night as the week comes to a close, it is time to sit down for half an hour and decide what will happen over the following seven days. Some suggestions of what you would schedule in:

- Enter work times and any work-related appointments so that you can fit everything else in around that
- Housework that needs to be completed in the next week (which day and how much time you are going to spend)
- Planning of the meal menu for the week (which day and time will you focus on that)
- Food shopping (day and time to get it done and stick to just what you need in relation to what you are going to cook)
- Any activities with family and friends that you will need to attend
- Exercise schedule (what day, time, what type of exercise, and for how long will you exercise)
- Weigh in days with expected and actual weight (this you will determine depending on what you have set as your goal)
- Reward for the week if you achieved what you planned (write in what that reward would be and when you will have it)

- Any study time or reading you would like to do
- Important phone calls that you need to make
- Bills that need to be paid (day and what it is)
- Private time with your partner just to hang out (book in date nights regularly). We tend to get so busy this part gets put in the back burner and is often overlooked

Now that you have entered all your commitments for the next week, quickly look at your next day and make a mental note of what is booked in. This is a great strategy to avoid overwhelming, and it lets you just focus on the tasks that need doing on that day. Each day, as you are completing your tasks, it feels great to tick them off as you go along and gives you a sense of closure and achievement. If you miss out on doing a particular task, carry it over in the evening to another day in that week or decide whether it is a huge priority that must be attended to.

Your diary will hold you accountable to yourself. Soon, you will become more effective about your days, and it will be easier to cope with everyone and everything. Give yourself a break and forget about your diary on your free days and during holidays. You deserve to just do as you please, and this is a great reward for all the great work you are already doing. You might also start finding extra spare time now that you are more organised and efficient.

What If?

I know that by this stage you have a lot of questions you would like answered. So here is a list of questions and answers that may be on your mind:

Q. Kids are a huge distraction and things often don't go as planned. How do I overcome this and stick to my daily tasks?

A. It is important that our children see us as role models. In this case, we want to show them that being organised can be easy, fun, and they get to do a lot more as a result of it. I have had my child on a routine since he passed the newborn stage. The bedtime routine was typed up on his nursery wall for everyone to follow so that he had consistency and structure just before going to sleep. Just to illustrate a point, I would like to elaborate a little bit more on this story.

As we know, newborns cannot be taught a routine. From about four and a half months on, this is the best thing for babies. My husband and I were seriously sleep deprived for an eight-week period between our son's age of two and half months to four and a half months. We were so desperate for a solution that we went as far as booking into sleep school. Judd would only sleep fifteen to twenty minutes at a time. We were like walking zombies. I remember looking at people around me and wondering if they had a good night's sleep. That's all I wanted because I felt like I was up 24/7.

One day, my mum and I were shopping in a local shopping centre and we went into a book store. It clicked into my head to check if there was a baby sleep section in the store so I could see if I could pick up some tips and strategies to get Judd to sleep for anything longer than fifteen minutes at a time. Well, there were probably twenty to thirty book titles all on baby sleep and different ways and systems of getting your baby to sleep through the night. How do I choose which one is best?

I spent thirty minutes browsing through all of them and changing my mind along the way. I was stuck! And then out of nowhere, I noticed a red star on one of the books that promised me 'Results in less than five days' Woo hoo! I loved it. Don't you love when you see these simple and easy promises on books—especially for weight loss? They work wonders. It's in our human nature to want things in a list and as simple as possible. Ninety per cent of books are purchased purely on the title. However, also, 90 per cent of books are not even read past the first chapter and acted upon the recommendations shared by the author. You are doing well to have gotten as far as getting here, so stay with me. I promise you it will be worth your time.

I have a belief that you can take away some gold from every book, person, and situation. It is how you decide to put all those things together that will define your journey to success!

So back to my baby sleep story. I obviously purchased the book that promised quick results! We went home, and the moment I walked in, pen in one hand, book in the other, I started reading. I had to find out the secret (just like you are right here) and put it into action asap. My mum was in charge of babysitting for the afternoon so that I could get all this information and set it all up. It took me just under twenty-four hours to get it read, type out the programme, and explain it to my husband, who also was in the process of reading it after me.

"Those who make the worst use of their time are the first to complain of its shortness."

Jean de La Bruysre

We had a spreadsheet, a clock that lit up when you pressed a button so you could see the time in the dark, and armed with a strong will and attitude, we were ready to start. We decided that I would be in charge Night 1 and him the following on. We would then alternate and see what happens over the next five days. The book suggested that at the same time you can wean the baby from the breast and had a system of how to do this as well. I thought, 'Why not kill two birds with one stone?'

Night 1 was the worst. Judd woke up fifteen to twenty times and would stay awake anywhere from fifteen to forty-five minutes at a time. I was exhausted of getting up, watching the clock, and noting down times and intervals. But I was determined to stick it out and really test the system over the promised time frame. Follow the instructions 100 per cent and be strong. In the morning, both Judd and I were so exhausted—we had been through one of the roughest nights and we spent most of the day napping.

Night 2 was ten times easier. Judd only woke up four times and settled much faster. Gee, these babies learn fast. Night 3, he woke up only once, and by Night 4, he was weaned from his night-time feeds and sleeping right through the night! Success! We were so excited and proud of sticking it out for a few days. This resulted in us having great sleep and free time every evening after 8 p.m. Of course, we continued with the same routine and stuck to the system permanently. It didn't seem like a chore. It was easy, step by step. Even the grandparents followed and were often reprimanded by us if we caught them doing something different.

I travelled with Judd for three months alone at the age of seven months. During this time, we visited seven countries in four continents, and he had to be put to sleep in so many unfamiliar places and beds. Every day was different and exciting, but the bedtime routine was always the same. We adjusted wherever we went, and everyone was so impressed by how a baby his age always slept at a certain time every single day and never whinged or cried when left to fall asleep.

Now that he is a bit older, we are starting to encourage habits such as putting things away—not just his stuff but helping as much as he can with the household tasks—even though he just turned two. He learns from his role models that everyone needs to participate. That makes the job easier for everyone, and then we have more time for fun and interaction.

It is not too late to start, even if your children are not babies. Show them and be an example of what you would like them to become. It will make your life easier, and they will show a lot more respect towards you. Persist and stick to what you need to have in order for your life to also be easier and more enjoyable. Show them that being organised is a great way to get more done and have more time for fun without any guilt.

I really hope you got the moral of this story. In any new challenge or situation that you don't like, you need to find out or research how to fix it. Then you take the information and follow it precisely. It won't feel natural or easy to begin with, but over time, new habits will form, and you will unconsciously be doing what once felt so difficult.

Q. What happens if I have an emergency and cannot get my set of tasks completed for the day?

A. There is no need to panic in this situation. You can always open you diary and shuffle a few things around so that the stuff you missed out on gets completed over the next few days. A suggestion would be to add one task from that day to the following three to four days so that it gets spread out and easier to finish off. You will be surprised once you start this that some days you may feel extra motivated that things are running smoothly, you end up doing lots in just that one day.

Q. There are just way too many tasks and appointments in my schedule. How do I fit it all in? I feel like all I do is go from one task to another.

A. Delegation and prioritisation. By getting the whole family involved in what needs to be done, your list should be reduced. If you haven't delegated up until now, start by having a family meeting to explain that you need more help around the house. Set some new rules and work out a chores chart. This way, everyone will know what their role and jobs within the household are. Have rewards for the kids and even your partner if they are sticking to the new rule and doing a good job. You can also decide what you will take away as a luxury from them if they do poorly. Family meetings are a great way to catch up with everyone and discuss frustrations in an open and supportive environment. That way, any unplanned outburst of frustration will be reduced amongst everyone involved. It will make your family stronger and more united. The family meeting time can be scheduled every week into your diary, and it can also be the time you use to coordinate your diary with everyone's schedule.

Remember that you need to look after yourself before you can look after anyone else.

The second one is prioritisation. Work out what are the most important tasks at the moment that will move you closer to your goals. Perhaps the house does not need to be vacuum cleaned every single day. Sometimes your priorities will come first over the other members of the family. You shouldn't feel guilty if you need to say 'no' to loved ones from time to time and take some 'me' time. You are not a bad or uncaring person if you sometimes worry about yourself first.

Q. What if I start using the diary because it is a new and shiny idea, but then I get bored and quit? I am back at square one just like I've started and stopped many diets in the past.

A. The secret is to never quit quitting. Just like a recent advertisement on TV encourages smokers 'To never quit quitting', I would suggest to you that you use this powerful statement in anything you find challenging to stick at. It may mean that you just haven't found your system of doing something in a sustainable way. However, from the moment you decide that you will succeed at something and you fully believe it, your unconscious mind will start work towards moving you to the destination of your choice.

Easy Reference Guide on How to Get Better Organised:

1. Write out your menu plan for the week and shop according to it. You are more likely to stick to it, and the money you will save will be just a bonus.
2. Book in your exercise times as if they are an appointment you need to attend. This way, cancellation is less likely.
3. Use a diary to schedule in exercise, food shopping, and times for other activities that you want to accomplish. Once you write it down, your unconscious takes ownership of the tasks set out.
4. Plan your week ahead on Sundays (if you can involve your family in this, it will help you to be held accountable when you want to deviate from the schedule).

5. Make sure you schedule in some down time and fun activities as a reward for your commitment to your goals.
6. Never shop on a hungry stomach—the temptation to buy unhealthy stuff will be too hard to resist.
7. Don't keep tempting treats in your pantry. If they are not there, you won't be able to have them even if you feel like it. Keep healthy snacks instead and have them in weak moments.
8. Write out and review your goals regularly to keep focussed and be able to reassess any alterations you need to make to them.
9. Share the cooking and preparation of lunches with everyone in the family. This makes it less of a chore, and it's more fun being together during the preparation and eating of meals. Think of it as quality time to talk about the day instead of spending it in front of the TV.
10. Perform a time audit of what you actually spend your time on each hour of each day. This will give you a really clear picture of where you may be wasting time and how you can turn it into an opportunity to either shop, exercise, or spend time with the family and so on.

De-clutter Your Home, Handbag, and Wallet

To make getting organised easier to maintain and sustain, it is important that you also put into action 'Mission De-clutter'. Refer to Appendix D for a template on this. The benefits of this are not to be underestimated. Bring back the value in what you have, and only keep what you use. The three main areas I would suggest starting are:
1. The Kitchen—go through the pantry and throw out all expired supplies. Then clean out your fridge and organise everything so it is easy to find. The last step is to clean out all the drawers and spots where dust and dirt collects. Set aside one whole day to do this.
2. The Bathroom—remove and dispose of any products you haven't used for the past twelve months, especially if they have already been opened. The reason for this is because whatever ingredients they had that were active before opening are now useless because when the product is exposed to air or oxygen, its effectiveness decreases over time.
3. The Wardrobe—this is one that is most difficult for a lot of people. I can guarantee you that if you haven't worn an article of clothing

in the past twelve months, you are probably not even aware that it still exists in your wardrobe. And since you are now on the way to becoming slimmer, you don't need to be hanging on to old clothing that once was used to hide your body away.

Actually, what I would recommend as a fantastic reward for yourself once you have reached your goal weight is to invest some money into getting styled by a professional stylist and start fresh with your wardrobe pieces. A stylist will teach you what is best for your body shape, what colours are most flattering on you, and where to shop for quality pieces that can be used in a variety of ways so that you have a versatile wardrobe for a fraction of the price.

The benefits of doing this are priceless and include:

1. Feeling confident about yourself
2. Loving how the new clothes make you feel
3. Projecting a certain and confident persona to others
4. Creating outstanding first impressions
5. Having more space in your wardrobe
6. Spending less money on random pieces of clothing
7. Investing in quality that lasts more than one season
8. Having clothes that flatter your size and shape
9. Learning to accessorise, mix, and match for many looks

Once you have dealt with the big three key areas to de-clutter, it's time to move on to your office, filing cabinet, other drawers, and shelves. Use the template provided in Appendix D to help you plan out your 'Mission De-clutter'. If you live with other people, get everyone involved. Remember the good old saying: 'Many hands make light work.' You may be finished in half or a quarter of the time if everyone was assigned a specific area of the home.

As you finish with your home or even before you begin, take care of de-cluttering your handbag and wallet. These two items tell a lot about the value we place on ourselves. The most successful people invest a good amount of money into these items and keep them spotless. Use only one credit card that gets paid off monthly, do not have receipts floating around, and have cash (lots of it) always on hand. This does not mean you have to spend this cash, but having it will attract more in your life. A great tip that was shared with me is to plan daily what you would spend the cash on and write it down. This will become a reality the more you do it, and you will actually start having the money to spend.

Now you have more room to think, move, and include in your life. *Out with the old and in with the new!* There will be no distractions and true value for what is left. You will feel wonderful, refreshed, and ready to take on any new challenge. Make a start by taking out some rubbish bags and boxes. Then move on to the next action and so on.

Top 3 Tasks to Be Completed from This Chapter:

1. Perform a time audit for the next two weeks, breaking down each day into one-hour blocks.
2. Buy a diary, start using it, and hold a family meeting to discuss and coordinate schedules.
3. De-clutter you home, handbag, and wallet.

Chapter 3

Ultimate Weight Loss Secret 3: The Four Levels of Critical Thinking and the Six Core Human Needs

> The trouble with most people is that they think with their hopes or fears or wishes rather than with their minds.
> (Will Durant)

Four Levels of Critical Thinking

Learning this concept and how true it is in how we get results in life was monumental in my own development and self-awareness. I realised why sometimes I would progress whereas other times I would be stuck in the same position for months on end. It is very important to understand that these levels of thinking apply in all areas of life. They can be used to move you forward by asking yourself the simple question: 'What level of thinking am I operating out of right now?'

Level 1 thinking is what I have named *mastery*.
Level 2 thinking is the *stretch/learn zone*.
Level 3 thinking is the *comfort zone*.
Level 4 thinking is *self-sabotage*.

The Quality of Our Lives Is Determined by the Amount of Level 1 Experiences We Can Collect

Level 1

An example of Level 1 thinking would be someone that enjoys running and does it regularly and consistently over time. For this person, getting up and performing this task is a joy, and they get a huge rush from the activity.

Even if it's raining outside, you see them jogging along the side of the road and wonder how they can be bothered exercising in those conditions. This person cannot imagine their life without going for a run at least five days in a week. It's set as a habit, and it never feels like they are forcing themselves to do something they don't like.

So Level 1 thinking is doing what feels good, and it is also good for you, others, and the greater good. It is a level where you are near mastery and you are performing tasks at an unconscious level. No one ever reaches mastery since there is always more you can learn about something. Perhaps this runner hasn't managed a 100-km marathon. That would be the new level of mastery he/she can aspire to.

Level 2

Whenever we are searching for new results or outcomes in life, this is the level we need to be operating out of. The only way to mastery is via Level 2 thinking which is: doing what doesn't feel good, but it is good for you, others, and the greater good. This is where I would like to spend more time explaining how you can use this in your life to achieve the changes you are looking for.

Learning and stretching is not meant to be comfortable. It is only at the point of confusion that you are on the cusp of learning something new. So in the process of losing weight and becoming a new, healthier, and fitter version of you for life, you need to accept that things are not going to feel comfortable and easy.

Having the awareness and knowledge that this is the path you need to follow and persist with will ultimately get you to Level 1 thinking, where you end up finding your new lifestyle simple, easy, and lots of fun.

There is no need to jump into massive action in every aspect of making a change in your lifestyle. Break it down into different sections, where you focus on one thing at a time for a period of time until it becomes easy. Then you add on another and another and so on. For example, if you have never been a person to eat breakfast, start off with having a healthy breakfast every single day until such time that you can't even imagine starting your day without it. Some other activities and suggestions include:

- Not eating sweets
- Having a healthy lunch
- Exercising 'x' amount of days per week
- Using your diary to get organised
- Cutting out full sugar drinks and having mostly water
- Preparing and taking your lunch to work every single time
- Not eating any carbohydrates past lunch time
- Having healthy dinners (protein and vegetables combination)
- Planning your menu plan for each week and shopping regularly according to this plan

All of the above are habits that rarely exist amongst overweight/obese people. The great thing about making them part of your lifestyle is that not only will you be more organised, lose weight, and get fit, but also you will definitely save money by pre-organising menu plans and taking lunches to work. What could you do with all that spare cash?

The bottom line is that it takes action and persistence to make changes that don't feel good but are good for us in the long run. Remember that the only way out of a rut is to start thinking at Level 2.

Level 3

Most of our life is spent right here at Level 3—doing what feels good, but it's not good for us, others, or the greater good. The comfort zone is a very alluring place to live. People often get stuck here and wonder why is it they are not moving forward in life—this could be work, health, or relationships.

So what does this mean in weight-loss terms? Well, basically, if you continue doing what you have been doing because it's familiar and comfortable, you will continue getting what you have been getting—a person stuck at a large weight with huge health risks that may result in a shorter life.

Break out of this level if you want to bring about changes in the way you live. Step out of the comfort zone and show everyone that you are willing to take a risk and put yourself out there to try new strategies and tips that may work for you. You won't always hit the jackpot, but having the flexibility to take any setbacks as feedback, your next attempt will get you a step closer to the desired outcome you are looking for.

Level 3 thinking holds you back and keeps you stuck. Your ego lives here and speaks to you in ways to keep you away from harm. This may have been useful in the caveman days, but today, we must keep learning and improving ourselves in order to achieve high quality lives where we feel happy and fulfilled in all areas.

Level 4

When things start getting out of hand, it is usually a sign that you are spending time at Level 4 thinking—doing what doesn't feel good, it's not good for you, others, or the greater good. Self-sabotage is very destructive, and in the long run, it can lead to anxiety or depression.

Eating chocolate to the point that you cannot have anymore or you are ready to throw it up is neither pleasant nor good for your well-being. Procrastination is something I would also put at this level. Most of the time, people are aware they are procrastinating, and this does not feel good to them nor is it good for them.

Level 4 thinking is a scary place to be, and often people stuck here are crying out for help because of the despair they are experiencing in their lives.

● ● ●

Now that you have a more detailed understanding of the four levels of critical thinking, you can start examining how you tackle everyday life. My challenge to you is to write down three Level 2 activities in your diary prior to the start of a new week and follow through on them within that week. It's not meant to feel good, but you will start seeing changes within yourself in a very short period of time.

The Master Dabbler Pattern

Have you ever wondered why you lose a bit of weight, feel good for a little while, only to put it back on and revert back to your old habits? I often hear people come to me and say, 'I've tried this and tried that, but nothing has worked for me. I have lost all hope that I can ever be my ideal weight.' This is where I can very clearly illustrate to you the reasons for this using the four levels of critical thinking.

When I originally learnt about the Dabbler Pattern, an example of how someone learns to play tennis was shared with me. So I would like to use that as the example here as well, after which we can relate it back to weight loss so you can get an understanding where you may be going wrong.

When you make a decision to learn something new, you expect that there will be challenges ahead. In this case, imagine you are a person that has never played tennis before. You go out, buy all your gear, and hire a coach that will train you. The first step is to learn how to hit the ball. In the beginning, it may seem impossible, especially if you are not that good at hand-eye coordination. You persist, get encouraged, get some great advice on what you can change, and through your Level 2 thinking (which, as we know, is doing something that doesn't feel good but is good for you), you finally master the art of hitting a tennis ball over the net.

Hitting the ball then becomes Level 1 thinking (doing what feels good and is good for you). You then reach a fork in the road. Do you continue playing or stop? If you decide to continue playing, the next thing you may learn is how to serve the ball. So it starts again. Level 2 thinking is doing something that doesn't feel good but is good for you. Once again, with the help of your coach, your own persistence, and determination, you continue practising until such time that you start feeling good serving, and it also becomes Level 1 thinking of doing what feels good and is good for you.

At each step, you reach a fork in the road and must make a decision whether to continue or stop playing tennis. If you continue, you then take on another skill that you must persist and work at before mastering it so it becomes unconscious and natural to you. At one point in all of this, you will reach a major fork in the road which usually occurs in every challenge or new learning. In our example of playing tennis, that major fork in the road would be the point where you need to decide whether you continue and turn professional or stay an amateur and only play socially.

If at any step along the journey your decision is to quit or stay with whatever feels comfortable, then you start dabbling in Level 3 thinking (doing what

You and I are not what we eat; we are what we think.
Walter Anderson

feels good, but it's not good for you). If you continue down that path, you start dabbling in un-resourceful behaviour, which is Level 4 thinking, and you move further away from improving in your skills and getting the lifestyle you were so motivated to have at the very beginning.

Becoming and staying fit and healthy requires you to move through the exact same steps as the example of learning to play tennis. Each time you persist through an unfamiliar and uncomfortable habit (for example, eating healthy or exercising regularly), you will reach a point where these activities become easy to do and very much feel good at the same time.

This is where a lot of people go wrong in weight loss. They practise Level 2 thinking for a little while or until such time that they have mastered a few skills in having a healthy lifestyle. However, as each fork in the road approaches, they must make a decision to continue or just revert back to the old habits. These habits are very much about the comfort zone of Level 3 and the self-sabotage of Level 4.

Knowledge is power! Having the understanding and awareness that this is what is happening will help you in catching yourself in moments of weakness. If you slip up, it's OK because you can always reverse the process and start climbing up those steps of Level 1 and Level 2 just by changing your actions and most of all your thinking. It is never too late, and armed with these skills, you will achieve your weight loss goals a lot faster.

Six Core Human Needs

Having an understanding of human behaviour and what drives us is one of the most important aspects in realising why you are stuck at your current weight. The six core human needs were originally defined by Anthony Robbins, and to this day, they play a major role as to how each of us meet them. These needs are universal amongst all people. There is only one difference—whether we meet them un-resourcefully or resourcefully.

Depending on how we satisfy these needs will determine our experience of happiness. They describe why we do what we do and why we don't do what we know we should be doing. Either way, we end up fulfilling these needs in one way or another. So here they are:

Core human need 1: Certainty

Also could be named safety, sameness, comfort, or control. In weight loss terms, people tend to meet this particular need un-resourcefully. This could be by watching TV for hours instead of having a life, food, control of others, routine (one that is holding you back), or procrastination.

To meet the need for certainty in a resourceful way that is sustainable, you would begin with having certainty in yourself, backing yourself no matter what, allowing yourself to become who you need to become in order to handle your problems, or having routines that support and provide a foundation for excellence.

The need for certainty and comfort may sound like a cosy place to be. What do you think would happen if you were always certain of what was going to happen and you had no variety or surprises about anything in life? Extreme boredom! This is exactly what most people want to avoid. It can result in creating a feeling that you are stuck and not moving or growing past the point where you are at now. I couldn't think of anything worse. That's why there are six core human needs common for all of us—to keep us engaged, interacting with others, and loving all the surprises and challenges life throws at us.

How do you think you are meeting your need for certainty?

Core human need 2: Uncertainty

This can also called variety or adventure. We need to have both in order to create a great life balance. An un-resourceful way of meeting this need would be doing overwhelming things—drug taking, changing TV channels, getting drunk, self-sabotage, or creating drama and problems for ourselves for no good reason.

Some resourceful ways of meeting this need would be to have different hobbies, new challenges, be creative and playful, embracing adventure, or having a great ability to change the meaning of an event so that it sits with you a lot better (this is also called a 'reframe' in coaching terms).

'Variety is the spice of life' as the saying goes. Often, people that have too much certainty in their lives could bring on variety by creating drama in their relationships, finances, and even health. A mentor of mine once told me that his wife fulfilled her need for variety by watching daytime drama series. By seeing other people go through the ups and downs in a particular show and following that on a regular basis, she fulfilled her need for uncertainty. I must say that is a healthy way of taking care of that need, since their relationship was very loving, supportive, and instead she was not taking her need for uncertainty out on their marriage.

What are the things that you do to meet your need for uncertainty?

The following two needs are the needs of the personality.

Core human need 3: Significance

Usually, people that like to be getters of significance meet this need unresourcefully by putting others down, gossiping, telling sad stories about themselves, being promiscuous, playing the martyr or victim, lying in a way that gets them caught, or being rebellious. Anorexia is a destructive way of acquiring significance. Mass murderers do this is in a very toxic way. And obtaining material possessions is a very fleeting way of getting to feel significant.

Resourcefully meeting this need, you can practice being the leader of self and others, do volunteer work, speak up for yourself, achieve your set goals, and become the master in your field of endeavour. For example, get involved in a cause and practice giving others huge value.

This particular need can also be classed as one of the most powerful needs that everyone strives to fulfil. We all want to feel that we matter and that we are important. It can often be the need that is a prime motivator for most people that drives their actions, decisions, and behaviour. Our society is designed for us to always be climbing the ladder of significance, and it shuns insignificance out of the way. With significance comes self-esteem and pride, which are important elements of pleasure.

Significance is one of those things that you should always focus on giving. By giving it, you will get it in return without fail. The Law of Reciprocity says that if you give, your needs will be taken care of as well.

Are you a getter or giver and getter of significance?

Core human need 4: Love/Connection

In the absence of love, we will settle for connection. When someone meets their need for love un-resourcefully, they come across as being needy, often may harm themselves, and they usually have unhealthy relationships or seek for connection through problems such as drugs, alcohol, and so on.

A sustainable way of meeting our need for love and connection includes being a person that shares, is supportive, connects through nature, self, and knows their self-worth and truth.

Love is the most powerful emotion there is. Everything we do is to fulfil this need for love and connection. The three fears we all have revolve around this concept of love: the fear of not being good enough, not being loved, and not belonging. It's ingrained in us from the day we are born.

I remember reading about a study whereby an army of babies were going to be raised to act as soldiers for a particular country. These babies were purely brought into this world for military purposes, and the nurses that looked after them were instructed to give them their milk every four hours and nothing else. It was very sad and at the same time very interesting what happened. This illustrates how important this core human need is. Since these babies were not given any love, touch, or affection, they all died from not having this need fulfilled. The experiment had a devastating outcome. It proved how important and crucial love is from the very beginning to our survival.

Where do you fit in when you think about how you meet your need for love and connection?

The last two core human needs are the needs of the spirit. They are contribution and growth. Here, our need for contribution is met by us doing something for others or the community without personal gain. The need for growth would be met by learning and developing ourselves to become the best version of ourselves so we can move through the different levels of consciousness and develop into high quality individuals. The more we are driven by contribution and growth, the more we are likely to help and inspire others to do the same. For example, the Dalai Lama is the only person in the world that at this moment in time is driven by these two needs the most.

Working out what your two core drivers are

Knowing what your two core drivers are will get you to your desired outcomes a lot faster. This is especially when you start meeting them resourcefully. To work that out, get a friend to help you with this exercise. To elicit your two core drivers, they need to ask you about your global beliefs. Global beliefs are all about things that are external to us. For example: 'Women are . . . , men are . . . , Australia is . . . , my job is . . . '

Get your friend to ask you these questions very quickly. You need to answer the first thing that comes to mind about the question. If you get stuck, get your friend to change the question and move on. The whole exercise needs to be done fairly quickly with lots of questions. At the same time, your friend needs to also be writing down your responses so that later on you can look at the answers, which will reveal which two core needs are your key drivers. When analysing the answers, work out which of the needs they are linked to the closest.

Going forward knowing your core drivers will give you the edge in understanding what moves you forward and whether that need is being met resourcefully.

Addictions

If a certain activity is met by three or more of the core human needs, then it is an addiction. Addictions can be good or bad. The more needs that are being met, the bigger the addiction. The reason you have an addiction is because it fulfils most, if not all, of your needs. An addiction is just a vehicle to fulfil your needs. If you lose it, know that you will find another vehicle to replace it.

Another way to understand how our core human needs are met is amongst the people we are with. If you are with someone that satisfies two of your needs, you have a connection. If they satisfy four of your needs, then you have a bond. And if six of the core needs are being met by someone, then they will never want to leave you.

> The man who knows where he is going the world makes way.
> (Napoleon Hill)

Top 3 Tasks to Be Completed from This Chapter:

1. Write down three activities you will do in the next week that are Level 2 thinking and do them.
2. Work out how you are meeting your six core needs. Are there some that you are meeting un-resourcefully? If yes, how can you flip this so that you begin meeting them resourcefully and sustainably?
3. Get some help from a friend to help you elicit your two core drivers.

CHAPTER 4

Ultimate Weight Loss Secret 4: Language

> Choose a positive, cheerful, confident attitude and see how your world changes for the better!

We experience our world by the language that we use. Language is very powerful, and our unconscious mind is always listening to everything we say to ourselves internally and externally. From this, it brings about into our reality everything we think and talk about. After all, we are what we think and talk about.

Half of what we communicate with others is via the words we say and the tone we use when saying them. So other people's perception of us and the response we get from them is hugely related to our ability to be effective communicators. *The meaning of a communication is the response that it gets.* This is a very powerful NLP presupposition (a linguistic assumption), which I will get into in more depth later on.

Even just changing something as simple as your answer to the everyday question 'How are you?' will make you feel different and others more responsive and open to communication. Rather than just saying, 'Good' or 'Good, thanks', answer with responses like 'Fantastic', 'Excellent', or 'Really well, thank you'.

In addition to using those types of responses, add a bit of spice in the tone of voice you answer in. Saying fantastic is great, but if you say it in a low, boring tone of voice, it will still come across as fake and your actions and tone will definitely speak louder than your words. Ninety-three per cent our all our communication is body language and tonality. Get yourself in an upbeat state even if you don't feel like it. In the beginning, it may feel awkward, but the saying 'Fake it till you make it' rings true here, because soon, you will be able to choose your state and how you communicate with ease. The most successful people have this unbelievable ability to call upon any state they need to get the results they are looking for in life, business, or relationships.

The next thing I would like you to notice within yourself is how you communicate with yourself and others in regard to the things you do or don't want in your life. Are you speaking in a moving away language or moving towards language? Moving away language means expressing what you don't want in life. An example of this is: 'I don't want to be lazy'. Moving towards language is when you express what you want. An example of this is: 'I want to be fit and healthy'.

It is important to know that our unconscious mind does not process negatives. That means it doesn't hear 'don't', 'can't', 'won't', and so on. If you are consistently using moving away language, you are actually attracting more of what you don't want in your life. So in the previous example of 'I don't want to be lazy', saying this over and over again will only bring about more laziness and lethargy in your life. Remember to state your desired outcomes as you want them, because chances are, they have a higher probability of coming to fruition when they are spoken this way.

Some other words of phrases to avoid include:

'I am confused'—replace this with 'I need some clarity around this'
'No worries' or 'No problem'—replace it with 'Too easy'
'Try'—replace it with 'Do'
'But' or 'However'—replace it with 'And'
'I don't want to feel pain'—replace it with 'I want to be healthy and strong'

Always Say It as You Want It and It Will Be Manifested!

A Great Empowering Vocabulary Results in Outstanding Outcomes

Since words reflect how we experience the world and language creates our experience, having a rich vocabulary will also expand how you experience your world. Invest some time to learn new words and find out what something means if you come across it as an unknown. This alone will open up other doors of opportunity and interactions with different people. You may learn new ways of communicating and understanding how others communicate in order to bring about success and happiness in their lives.

Choosing and Entering a *State* of Your *Choice*

How we feel day today is a result of a choice we have made. Our state does not occur because of external factors. It is internal, and it happens when we make a decision to hold our bodies a certain way, speak in a particular tone of voice, and think of certain things what either make us happy, sad, elated, depressed, and so on.

To prove that this is the case, I would like you to go ahead and think of a time you were really sad. Go back to that time and see what you saw, hear what you heard, and feel what you felt. And as you think about that specific time that you felt sad, notice how you are feeling right now, at this moment. Is the feeling or state you are experiencing happy or sad?

The same exercise can be repeated about a time that you felt truly happy, and you can ask yourself the same questions as before. What came up for you?

You can see the power of this. Knowing this alone will help you through some tough times just by making a decision to enter a certain state and keep your thoughts in that direction, your body as you would when you access those feelings, and your words expressing exactly what is going on inside.

Please don't misunderstand that sometimes you may be in a really down and sad state due to unplanned circumstances. This may be a death in the family, someone being ill, or a break up of a relationship. It is completely natural to go through a grieving process when events such as these occur in our lives. The important thing to remember is that you can choose, after you have had time to grieve, how you will continue to feel and what states you will exhibit in front of others.

Neuro-linguistic Programming (NLP)

The study of NLP explores the relationship of how we think (neuro), how we communicate (linguistic), and our patterns of behaviour and emotion (programmes).

"Change your language and you change your thoughts"
Karl Albrecht

By studying these relationships, people can learn and transform how they traditionally think and act, adopting new and far more effective successful models of human excellence. I would strongly recommend having a read of some NLP books if you would like to study this powerful science of creating positive and effortless change in your life.

Some of the areas NLP can help you with include:
- Replacing negative emotions and behaviours into positive ones
- Removing phobias
- Transforming the way you go about everyday tasks, new strategies implementation
- Better understanding of your own needs, behaviours, and motivations and how to use this for a more positive impact in your life
- Eliminating certain foods from your diet, for example, if you eat a lot of chocolate and want to have less of it, NLP can help you achieve this
- Help to enhance and improve your interpersonal communications with those at home and at the office
- Eliminate a habit such as smoking with parts integration work
- Better understand other people's needs, behaviours, and motivations
- Become a better sales person or remove your fear of public speaking
- Be more successful at learning to influence your emotional and psychological states

The list could probably go on and on for a while longer. The benefits of learning and practicing NLP are outstanding, and not many people are aware of this new age way of creating positive change in their lives. Oprah Winfrey, Donald Trump, and Tom Cruise, just to name a few, are all students of NLP and actively use it in their everyday lives to improve their communication with themselves and, more importantly, their fans and associates. Once you have studied NLP, you become more aware of how widely used it is by so many successful people.

The other day, I was watching an episode with Chris Angel (he is a world famous mind-reader or as they call him, 'The Mind Freak'). He was about to put six girls into a trance and make them forget easy things such as their age and their name. It was really interesting to watch him do this with NLP language patterns and techniques. Having studied this science myself, I recognised what he was doing and how effective he was at putting these girls into a trance. This would not be possible with every single person. By picking highly suggestible individuals, you can do wonders just by saying a few words in a specific order and in a hypnotic tone of voice. The choice to change lies within the individual.

Words Shape Our Destiny

If we don't have a word for something, we cannot experience it. There was a story I once read that explained how Native American languages have no word for the word 'lie', because that word is not part of their language. It is also not part of their thinking and behaviour. So if we had no words for certain things, we wouldn't be able to understand the concept. Another tribe apparently had no words for 'hate', 'dislike', or 'war'.

Imagine not having words for furious, depressed, or hostile. Using those types of words will automatically put you in an un-resourceful state. Purge them from your vocabulary, and you will find that you start to experience the world in a different way.

My own business coach reminded me of this one day when I was using words such as 'pushing myself' and that 'I am under so much pressure' while I was speaking to him. No wonder that's exactly how I was feeling. Making the decision then and there to start using something as simple as 'I am doing this now and I will do that later' made the biggest difference in my inner balance, and I started feeling a lot calmer and at ease with everything I was planning to accomplish.

Changing your words may not necessarily alter the experience, but if it breaks your own emotional pattern, like it did for me, then everything changes. My perspective was different, and all of a sudden, I could take on even more than before. I now pass on this great knowledge to all of my clients as a way of paying it forward and creating shifts within them to feel more at ease and empowered to stay in more resourceful states.

Top 3 Tasks to Be Completed from This Chapter:

1. Work out what are some disempowering words that you use regularly and how you can change them to ones that are not so

un-resourceful. For example, you might like to change 'angry' to 'peeved' or 'argument' to a 'conversation'.
2. Consciously practice giving a different answer to the question 'How are you?' Notice how people seem and feel when you do that.
3. Practice choosing your state even if you don't start off feeling that way. Choose to do happy instead of sad and see what happens.

CHAPTER 5

Ultimate Weight Loss Secret 5: Diet

Nothing tastes as good as being thin feels.
(Author Unknown)

Every diet works! Whether or not it is sustainable by each person—that is something that would vary. Some diets are high in carbohydrates, and others are high in protein. Other diets eliminate all white foods, and some are very specific right down to which fruit and vegetables you are allowed to eat. What you like and eat most will result in whether a diet will work for you long term. When choosing to follow a particular diet, it is very important that you choose one that includes most of your favourite foods so that you can keep it up.

Often times, you will come across particular diets that are better for people with a hormonal imbalance or designed according to your blood group for optimum weight loss. These are all different systems that have been researched and have helped certain individuals. The trick is to find the right system for you. More than 90 per cent of people will have success with any diet they choose as long as they stick with it and follow the instructions rigorously. The ones that are doing all the right things but find that a diet is not bringing the desired results in weight loss should seek professional help first of all from their doctor, who will then refer them either to a specialist or perform tests to discover why the weight is not shifting with the plan.

The answer and solution to your weight loss woes is out there! You just need to invest some time, determination, and organisation to find your match that will keep you slim sustainably. It is like any challenge in life. It is only through trial and error that you will finally hit the jackpot and get the result you are after.

At this stage, you may say, 'But I have tried so many different diets and nothing seems to work!' I would like to ask you the following questions:

1. Was it the diet, or your lack of commitment to it?
2. Did you follow everything as specified, all of the time?
3. Did you combine exercise with your plan?
4. If you deviated from the diet, what would happen next?
5. How long did you give the diet a chance to see results?

Oftentimes, it is lack of commitment and making your own alterations to an eating plan that will bring unsatisfactory results. It is very important to follow the steps of a proven system, so that you have the highest chance of replicating other people's success with that diet/system.

Rule of Thumb for Most Healthy Eating

Here, I would like to take you through some very simple do's and don'ts for healthy eating. Most of this is common knowledge, but it is useful to repeat again.

Do's:

- Eat fresh, raw foods, such as fruits and vegetables
- Have a healthy breakfast with foods low in sugar
- Have three meals per day and two snacks all of the time
- Avoid carbohydrates after lunch
- Have protein to maintain muscle tone and keep you full
- Make your meals from fresh ingredients and from scratch
- Be active every single day
- Set an example for those around you by eating healthy

Don'ts:

- Eat processed foods and food that is in packaging for a long time
- Eat junk food just because it's easy and convenient
- Use too much oil, sugar, or salt in your cooking
- Eat big portions (keep your energy in less than energy out when losing weight)
- Let others eating habits influence yours

"People are so worried about what they eat between Christmas and the New Year, but they really should be worried about what they eat between the New Year and Christmas."

Author Unknown

- Make excuses or blame others for how you are
- Miss breakfast or have one or two meals per day only (this will only slow down your metabolism and speed up your weight gain)
- Fill your pantry with temptations (if it's there, you will want to have it)

80/20 Rule in Weight Loss

If there is something that you need to remember when planning on losing weight, it is this: 80 per cent of your weight loss will come from your diet and 20 per cent from your exercise. Remember the importance of energy in needs to be less than energy out in order for you to shed unwanted weight.

I have come across so many clients that are very active and enjoy exercise, however, they then think it is OK to eat more and have larger portions. Exercise should not be used as an excuse to eat more. If you don't like exercising, in the beginning, I would strongly suggest that you focus on getting your eating habits in order before adding activity to your new lifestyle. Partnered up together, they will give you optimum weight loss coupled with lots of energy and motivation to keep going until you reach your goal weight.

Weight Loss = 80% Focus on Diet + 20% Focus on Exercise

Weight Loss Journal

Never underestimate the power of having a detailed journal, where you record everything that goes into your body. Just like the time audit, the journal will reveal to you exactly what you are putting into your body and how much. If you haven't started your weight loss journal, I would strongly recommend completing a food journal for a couple of weeks so that you can have all the facts and truth in front of you. Eventually, this is what will keep you in line and accountable to yourself and anyone supporting you on this journey.

Keeping a journal can seem like a lot of work, but it is worth the exercise until such time that you are steadily seeing that your habits are changing and the weeks look stable with lots of progress.

Appendix A is a weight loss journal template that will help you with this.

Tips on How to Cut Down on the Junk

Takeaway nights should become a thing of the past. Just imagine all the empty calories, additives, and dodgy hygiene practices that are in a takeaway meal. Here are few ways to tackle the takeaway and junk-food-at-home temptation:

- Go through all the drawers and places you may keep takeaway menus. Rip them up and throw them out. Get rid of the temptation once and for all. Get the whole family to help as a symbolic gesture of you turning a new leaf in life towards a healthier lifestyle.
- Keep a jar in your kitchen so that every time you are tempted to buy takeaway, you end up putting away the money you would have spent. Just think about how quickly you will have some cash to put towards some nice new clothes when you have lost all that excess weight.
- When you walk past takeaway shops and you notice the smells, imagine being overpowered by the stench of vomit. Start to associate the old cooking oil smell with the smell of vomit, and that will break the habit. If you cannot do this, an NLP technique called 'Like to Dislike' can be applied to create this association in less than ten minutes.
- Often when tempted to eat junk food, it helps to ask yourself this question: 'At this moment, do I really want to eat this 'x' or do I want to be my ideal weight?' Your answer should really make you think about your actions.
- Don't buy any snacks for the pantry that would act as temptation. Give your family healthy alternatives instead. Fruit is a great substitute in the evening, when you may start getting those hunger pangs or desires to munch away at something. If this is you, perhaps save one of your two daily snacks for this time to subside your urge to cheat.
-

In moments that you are tempted to cheat . . .
It is important to distract yourself from the fantasies of the food you are so desperately craving. Here is a list of some distraction activities you can try out:

- Go for a walk
- Phone a friend

- Head to the gym
- Read a book
- Pamper yourself at home
- Dance to your favourite music
- Send an email
- Keep yourself occupied by doing a crossword puzzle
- Write in your journal
- Do some gardening
- Have a bubble bath

Top 3 Tasks to Be Completed from This Chapter:

1. Start writing everything you eat in your journal.
2. Get rid of all the junk food in your house including the fast-food takeaway menus.
3. Research a diet/eating plan that will fit your likes and is something that you see being normal eating for you in the long run.

Chapter 6

Ultimate Weight Loss Secret 6: Exercise

> Motion creates emotion.
> (Anthony Robbins)

How would you like to discover an easy and sustainable way to exercise from this day forward? I am here to explain a few myths around exercise and how it is possible to achieve your goal weight without the need to risk injury or other unpleasant side effects that rigorous exercise can bring on.

The first thing we need to clarify here are the differences between *health* and *fitness*. 'Fitness' is the physical ability to perform a particular athletic activity, whereas 'health' is the state where all the systems in the body are working in an optimal way. These two don't necessarily go hand in hand even though a lot of people are under the impression that one implies the other. It's great if you have both in your life, but having health first is always going to have bigger benefits in your life. What is the point of having a fantastic body if you don't live long enough to enjoy it?

To enjoy optimal health, you need to focus on training your *metabolism*. So how do you do this? Here, I would like to focus on and explain the difference between aerobic and anaerobic exercise and endurance versus power. Moderate exercise sustained over a long period of time using oxygen is called aerobic exercise. The aerobic system involves the heart, lungs, blood vessels, and aerobic muscles. By activating this system with the proper diet and exercise, it will start to burn fat as the primary fuel.

On the flip side, 'anaerobic' means 'without oxygen', and this type of exercise occurs when you produce short bursts of power. Instead of fat, you end up burning glycogen as the primary fuel, which causes the body to store fat. If your heart rate is lower, you are using the aerobic system, and if it is higher, the anaerobic system.

A lot of types of exercise can be either aerobic or anaerobic depending on the level of intensity you are performing them at. For example, walking, jogging, running, dancing, and swimming are all types of exercise that can be performed using either system. Playing tennis, basketball, badminton, and other similar sports are all anaerobic exercises.

Nowadays, our lives are filled with so many responsibilities, demands, and stress that a lot of people end up living a lifestyle filled with anaerobic exercise. So if the metabolism is constantly trained with anaerobic exercise, the burning of glycogen only continues. Once the levels of glycogen drop to a very low level, the secondary fuel that gets burnt is our blood sugar, which has an immediate effect on your health and vitality.

There are so many dangerous side effects when blood sugar levels drop, and just to bring your awareness around what those are, I have listed them below:
- Fatigue
- Exercise injuries
- Depression and anxiety
- Low blood sugar patterns
- Fat metabolism problems
- Premenstrual syndrome
- Circulation problems
- Stiff joints

Other things that have changed in today's world is the fact that our jobs have become less physical over the recent decades and reduced our physical activity day to day. To compensate for the inactivity we experience in everyday life, this thing we now call exercise was brought about. We all have a drive to produce the greatest results in short periods of time, however, this is often at the cost of our health and well-being. Rigorous exercise can actually make you less healthy and unlikely to result in a sustainable way of being active for life.

The secret here is to build a strong aerobic base for your body so you can train it for endurance and running more efficiently. By training your body to do all of this, you will soon discover that it is easier to burn off fat from your midsection, your immune system will be stronger, and you will feel more energetic and motivated to continue with physical activity on a daily basis. To create a strong aerobic base, you will need to get advice from a personal trainer or consultant as to how long they would recommend that you strictly only perform aerobic exercise. On average, the time frame would be somewhere between two to eight months.

After this period of aerobic exercise, a few bursts of anaerobic exercise can start to be introduced in your health and fitness regime. The purpose of the aerobic base is to train and teach the body how to deliver oxygen to every system and organ. When individuals push themselves hard to achieve their maximum heart rate, the body supplies blood and oxygen to the muscles which need it most. It omits the critical organs such as the liver or kidneys. By continuing this way of exercise, you can cause serious damage, weakness, and destruction to those organs. This is why warm-ups and cool-downs are such an important part of exercise and should not be forgotten each and every time.

The body will not burn fat unless you specifically train it to do so! The great thing about aerobic exercise is that it is not hard, tiring, or even risky to perform. You won't need to psych yourself up as much or worry if it's going to hurt for a few days later. This conditioning of your body to burn fat can result in the same type of metabolism that you may envy in others at this time.

Pitfall: Eliminating almost all fat in your diet won't necessarily reduce fat on your body!

This is very important to remember, because if anything, our bodies know really well how to throw themselves in 'emergency mode', where they begin to store fat more efficiently. This also applies in eating just one to two meals per day. Our bodies start to sense that there may be a lack of energy or fat coming in, and they start slowing down the burning process of these resources to ensure our survival going forward. I am often amazed at comments like: 'But I really don't eat all that much' or 'Everything I buy is light or low in fat.'

Change your focus: When you say you want to lose weight, what do you actually mean? Do you want to lose fluid from your body, muscle mass, or actual fat? Because depending on what types of exercise you perform, you will start losing one of those three. Losing water and muscle mass will not result in optimal health for you. In fact, you will find that the body will replace that very quickly, and you will be back to weighing even more than before.

The focus should always be on burning off the excess fat by performing aerobic exercise. So how do you know if you are performing aerobic exercise? The things to look out for are:
- Can you keep up a conversation while you are exercising?
- Is your breathing steady, audible, and not laboured?
- Does the exercise feel pleasurable but tiring?
- If you were to rate yourself on a scale from one to ten in terms of exertion, would you be around six to seven?

If you answered 'yes' to all of the above questions, you are most likely exercising aerobically.

In the beginning, you may need extra help in discovering exactly what your aerobic zone feels like. My suggestion to you would be to invest some money and buy yourself a heart-rate monitor. This will tell you exactly when you have entered your ideal aerobic exercise zone and whether you should increase or decrease your exercise intensity.

The best way to work out your aerobic exercise heart rate is by using this calculation:

180 - Your Age = Your Ideal Heart Rate (for aerobic exercise)

There are certain things to consider for particular individuals when calculating their ideal heart rate, and before beginning any exercise programme, it's best to consult your doctor. Alter your ideal heart rate in the following ways if you fit into any of these categories:
- If you are on medication or recovering from major illness, subtract ten points from your score.
- If you have been exercising for more than two years without any problems, add five points.
- If you have been exercising for up to two years without any problems, keep the score the same.
- If you have never exercised before, have an injury, and are prone to often get colds and flu, then subtract five points from your score.

"A man's health can be judged by which he takes two at a time—pills or stairs."

Joan Welsh

How Long to Exercise

Your aerobic exercise routine must have these three vital stages:

- Warm-up period of fifteen minutes. This is when you keep your hear rate at 50 per cent of your maximum heart rate. To work this out, use this formula: (220 - your age)/2 = 50% of your heart rate.
- Exercise within your aerobic exercise zone for at least twenty minutes, eventually working up to thirty to forty minutes.
- Take twelve to fifteen minutes to cool down properly by walking or some form of mild movement.

This type of exercise and workout will eliminate you linking it to pain every time you decide to exercise. If you just give it a go, you will soon discover that working out this way actually produces pleasure instead of pain, and your levels of energy and physical vitality will be something you have never experienced before.

You can also use the time while doing aerobic exercise as an opportunity to listen to motivational or educational tapes you are interested in, watch a favourite show, or the news. This way, you will feel like you have achieved a lot more in the space of an hour, and time restraints will be less of an issue. Be creative and alter the type of exercise you do to eliminate boredom.

Following your aerobic base training period...

Adding some anaerobic exercise will help you increase your muscle tone and produce more of the HGH (human growth hormone). This is responsible for keeping us younger. This hormone is naturally produced by our body until approximately the age of thirty. Women tend to continue producing it, and men stop altogether unless exercise is introduced to stimulate the production of this hormone. This is also the reason why women live longer. By doing short bursts of intense exercise, the production of HGH is stimulated, and those that are in their sixties, for example, will find that they can have the muscle tone and energy levels as in their twenties.

Incidental Exercise

Don't underestimate the importance of this, because it can literally change your life! It can also save you time in the long run when it comes to having a routine exercise schedule. Some ideas to get you started with your incidental exercise:

1. Take the stairs instead of the lift or escalator
2. If you take the bus, get off a few stops earlier, and walk the rest of the way
3. If you have a baby, go for walks and increase the intensity so that you can feel the workout
4. Turn your leisurely walks into power walks for a greater impact on your weight loss
5. Play with your kids in the park
6. Take your dog for a run
7. Park your car further and walk

Incidental exercise can also occur if you choose to get involved with teams and sports by making your spare time more active. If you are a social person and love meeting new people, a team sport is something you can participate in to satisfy your need for connection as well as have a workout that is a lot of fun. Joining a cycling group is a great way to drop a lot of weight quickly. Pick something that you enjoy and meet lots of new friends along the way.

Planning

Make a decision on what your exercise schedule will be, and plan it out in your diary around any other commitments. Make sure that you don't have more than two days rest between exercising. It is very important to build your aerobic base so that weight loss can occur in an optimum and healthy way.

Training Buddy

It is a well-known fact that having someone to do your exercise with is much easier, entertaining, and more motivating. Finding a training buddy is absolute gold! You won't want to let them down and neither will they. Together you will achieve your goals a lot faster.

Sharing your weight loss journey with someone you know is so rewarding for both yourself and them. In moments of weakness, it is unlikely that both of you will feel the same, and one will snap the other one out of the pit. In the end, you will both feel fabulous, healthy, and thankful to each other.

The Top 5 Benefits of Exercise

- Improved Immunity—regular exercise in your lifestyle will boost up your immune system, and you will be less susceptible to colds and flu than those who do not exercise.
- Elevated mood—the body produces the brain chemicals called endorphins through exercise, which in turn provide happy and pleasurable feelings.
- Lowered stress levels—just the opposite of the previous benefit, by having elevated moods via exercise, you will in turn be less stressed.
- Better sleep—research has shown that exercise provides the individual with more sound sleep at night.
- Increased energy—not only does exercise boost your metabolism, but it leaves you stimulated and fresh, ready to take on a lot more than if you are inactive.

Investing in a Personal Trainer

There is no faster way to get the results you are after than going to someone that is an expert in the field. Different people struggle with different areas in their weight loss journey. The three main ones are:

1. Diet—not knowing what's the right thing to eat (see a dietician).
2. Mindset—being stuck for years and not knowing how to start. To develop the self-awareness to achieve your goals and keep them sustainable for life, see a mindset coach like myself.
3. Exercise—no understanding of how to exercise properly (get a personal trainer).

These professionals will show you the correct way to exercise, eat, and think. It is especially important in the beginning to do a few sessions with a personal trainer so that you gain an understanding as to what exercise is best for you and how to do it properly. You might decide to do half your exercising with the trainer and half on your own. They will keep you accountable, and when you are paying someone for their time, you will be less likely to bail on them. A trainer will also push you that little bit harder than you would yourself, so knowing what that feels like will give you the ability to replicate it on your own.

Top 3 Tasks to Be Completed from This Chapter:

1. Work out your ideal heart rate for aerobic exercise and buy a heart rate monitor so you can start training in your aerobic zone.
2. Brainstorm all the different incidental exercise activities that you can do as part of your lifestyle and start doing them.
3. Plan your exercise schedule for the whole week—be creative and choose at least three different types of activities.

Chapter 7

Ultimate Weight Loss Secret 7: Mindset

If you don't like something, change it. If you can't change it, change your attitude.

(Maya Angelou)

Congratulations on getting this far into this life-changing book! It is now time for the best and most valuable chapter and insights I would like to share with you. This will, without doubt, enable you to have success on your journey to lose all the weight you want and start experiencing optimum health and vitality right now. If you are able to grasp and accept the following information, you will have results beyond your wildest imagination in all areas of your life. Perhaps you may think while reading this that it has nothing to do with losing weight—but don't be fooled by the simplicity of the concepts. I challenge you to think about them on a deeper level before discounting them as ineffective. It's time to talk about *choice*.

Who Chooses?

To make a change in your life, it always has to come by you choosing to create it rather than wishing and hoping it will happen by chance. In all my extensive study of human behaviour, I have come to realise that all responsibility is mine for my life and results. I am the one driving my bus all of the time. As a coach and a mentor, I cannot make anyone do anything unless they are the ones that have chosen to do it.

My clients come to me because they have a problem that needs solving and they don't know how to do it themselves. They are very emotionally involved in the situation and cannot see the whole picture on their own. I act as a disassociated observer and see that often the solution is not in the problem, but something that is not being said consciously. Albert Einstein once shared a quote with us that 'A problem cannot be solved with the same logical level of thinking.' Coming from a place of understanding, love, and commitment to serving an individual get through their challenges and frustrations is very rewarding and inspiring to me. When I see my clients grow as we spend time educating, sharing metaphors, and insights along the way, it gives me a sense of achievement that I have been able to pay forward all the education and insights I have collected along the way.

Make a decision today that you are the one driving your bus and be empowered with the knowledge that any change is possible. Go for want you want and take the actions to make it real. All the resources you need are within you right now, and there is no reason to wait any longer to make a start.

But What If . . .

I don't have the time right now to do it—if you don't have the time right now, you never will. To create any change, we can only be motivated by either extreme pleasure or extreme pain. There is no in between! You either want something so badly (for example, to become a famous singer) or the situation you are in currently is damaging to your well-being (for example, you must lose weight to have optimal health). If there is no extreme pleasure or pain, you probably would have started and stopped creating your change many times over and failed. As a coach and a mentor, I help my clients to leverage as much pain or pleasure towards the thing that they want and move them to action so they get results a lot faster than if they were doing it on their own.

My partner or children restrict me from making the change—if you use an excuse such as this one, it is vital that you take a good look at how much value you place on yourself. The more you value yourself, the more others will respect and value you in return.

When it comes to your partner, you are there to be an equal and allow each other the room to grow. *The couple that grows together stays together!* If one of you does all the growing and the other one is left behind, it is very likely that the relationship will not survive the test of time for too long. Remember to have open communication and accept any issues you have with your partner as your problems and not theirs. This will open up the door to being able to resolve them yourself by changing how you feel or how you look at them.

A very powerful notion to remember if you decide to grow and expand your horizons to new possibilities is that in the beginning, those around you may not believe that you are capable of doing it. They will test you at first, but they will end up following once they see what is possible.

Your *tribe* will follow as you *grow*!

This is 100 per cent true and inspirational. I know from personal experience. Here, I would like to share my story with you so that you gain an understanding of how I know the above to be so true.

When I decided to embark on my coaching career, I was on my own and alone. I had big dreams and believed anything is possible. The road ahead was unknown, and I chose to remember, even before I made the decision to sign up for my education, what my mum always use to say to me, 'Every beginning is hard. You need to persist longer than you think to see the light at the end of the tunnel.'

She had repeated this to me time and time again, over the years growing up in Macedonia, and then again, when I moved continents, countries, cultures, and languages to the land of opportunity and now my favourite place to spend the rest of my life—Melbourne, Australia. I immigrated to Melbourne just after my fourteenth birthday as a confident, easy-going, and socially accepted teenager in my peer group back home. Life was very fast, fun, and social back home. We had the freedom to go out wherever we wanted and whenever we wanted without any supervision. Everything was close by, so parents didn't need to transport us from place to place, and living in the centre of the city gave us access to all the cafes, shops, and clubs that we would attend regularly up to a certain time for our age.

Arriving in Melbourne was quite a shock. After the initial excitement of being in a new country and seeing my mum after two and a half years apart, the realisation set in that I was imprisoned by the four walls of my room with the TV as my only companion and a school that I went to where nothing much fun was happening. And so it began—my two years of adaptation to this new culture, city, customs, and language. There were hundreds of times I wanted to go back to Macedonia. I cried about how lonely I felt, and I saw myself going backwards socially, since I had no one close to me that was my age that I could interact with and share my frustrations.

However, my mum knew. She knew I would be OK and settle in. She kept reminding me of how every beginning is hard and to keep persisting to find my own way to make it work. It took two years! In a teenager's life, that is an eternity. Looking back now at that time, I have to say those two years provided me with the time to become a great academic and a high achiever at high school. I won the overall achievement and contribution award three years running and really shone academically, having come from a country where we had studied most of the material being delivered in Australia, at a lot younger age. I was also doing it in a language I had not spoken before. I realise today that there was plenty of time to go out, socialise, and have boyfriends once I reached a level of maturity to get my licence and explore this beautiful country.

It was that experience that always reminds me of this: the road to change is often a lot slower than we would like it to be. It also carries a huge lesson within it, and if you were to look at it for what it is, it makes you the person you are today.

This is also what I remembered as I began my coaching journey. I must persist and do everything in my power to establish a coaching practice that I can run from home. That way, I can raise my brand new family and make sure my children get to have lots of different experiences, travel the world, and learn about different cultures. They will be able to create fantastic foundations and have the opportunity of creating empowering beliefs about what is possible.

The education takes time to become second nature, and surely enough, one day, bit by bit, things start to click into place and you gain momentum. The things that you have learnt become automatic and natural. So think of your change as a journey and not a destination to get to in the blink of an eye. That way, you will enjoy it a lot more and remember wherever you are at now is the very right time for you.

I feel like I will fail every time I start something new in weight loss—what you focus on is what you will get, to the exception of everything else. The unconscious mind is truly powerful in getting for us even things that we don't want. This is because it cannot process negatives. 'I don't want to fail' will simply be turned into failure by the unconscious mind. Focus on what you want and say it the way you want it all of the time. Learn to trust your unconscious, and it will bring about the desired outcomes you are after.

Self-worth

This is what this whole book has been about—the issue that is behind the problem. It has been very evident through my coaching and mentoring of my clients that the problem with being overweight, obese, or lack of exercise in their lives comes down to a single belief they hold about themselves—their lack of self-worth.

The value we put on ourselves is a huge indicator of what we think about ourselves. Why don't we see a vast amount of wealthy people being overweight? It is not because they have the money to have cooks, trainers, and dieticians that look after them. You can have all of that and still be overweight. The motivation and actions have to come from your internal view—how you feel about yourself and what value you put on yourself. Rich people know that their value and what they do in their community is huge, and they are usually very generous and giving with what they have. They support large charities and causes so that they can leave a legacy behind. Their passion goes far outside of themselves. They know if they help someone, they will be also taken care of in return. This is where the trust happens.

Focusing on serving rather than getting is the key. The person you need to start serving in the beginning is yourself and your body. Are you serving your body with energy that is clean, nourishing, and good for you? Are you serving your body with a good amount of activity that will keep it functioning at optimum?

If you take care of yourself, it will trickle down into other areas of your life.

Your first step is you. It has to be you. Others will notice the changes you are going through, and their mindset towards you will also change. They will start seeing the value you put on yourself and that you love yourself first before giving love to others. That's why a lot of mothers often will find it hard to lose weight after having children. Their immense love for their children changes their focus from themselves to their offspring.

"Attitude determines the altitude of life."
Edwin Louis Cole.

It is nature and nurture that cause us to want to protect and take care of our children to the best of our abilities. But there comes a time we also need to let go and allow them to start doing things for themselves and others around them. By not allowing this to happen, you may be creating beliefs in them that they are not good enough or can't do even simple chores. Parental love can sometimes smother and disable an individual when it comes to being able to function in adult life.

The years between zero and seven are the imprint period for children. It is during these years that all our beliefs about the world and us are created. Zero to three is the most powerful time as it is at this time that everything is egocentric, and by the time they hit five years of age, most beliefs are cemented. That's why it is important to always allow your children to help you when they want. You must also model for them the behaviours you want them to create for themselves. Just because they can't speak or express themselves well at this time, their unconscious is working overtime in collecting all the information that it finds to be true about the world and the people around.

Take care of your children, offer lots of love, support, and encouragement. Then trust and let go so they can find their own way and place in the world. This is going to empower them.

The greatest *gift* you can get from your children is their *independence* and the ability to stand on their own two feet.

You are the most important person in your life, so look after yourself and your body like a temple. After all, I am sure you would like to be around to see your children grow up and get involved in the activities they are a part of. Not only that, they will grow up to have respect for you and what you stand for. It's a win-win situation all round. They learn value and appreciation for what you have done and will go out into the world modelling what they have seen from you and their environment. You are not serving anyone by taking responsibility for everyone. In fact, you probably do that to fulfil your need for significance and hope that it will bring more love and connection your way.

The best way to get significance is by giving it to others. An example of this would be in trusting that others have all the resources available at this moment to achieve their dreams. They don't need rescuing by you. This will give them significance, and they will give it back by showing respect and admiration that you did not just let them off the hook. The love and connection will also come with the respect and admiration for your persistence and guidance. The feeling that you are their number one supporter that can see them achieve their desired outcomes is the most empowering feeling in the world to an individual, let alone a child.

When you work out where your low self-worth is coming from, this is what is going to make the difference in you having success on your weight-loss journey. Bring about awareness to your actions and self-talk to consciously change and turn your life around. Expand on your education, and this will expand your map of reality. What you are doing right now by reading this book is one of the steps towards your success. Read, research, and speak to people that are models of excellence in the field you want to succeed in.

Finding Mentors

If you want to be successful in business, you will need to find a mentor that is successful in business. If you want to have a fantastic relationship with your partner, then find a couple that already has this. The same thing goes for health and vitality. If you want to have this in your life, then find a mentor that already has this. The next step is to model what they do.

Modelling is the core of NLP and how we go about achieving outstanding results in the fastest way possible. It is not about reinventing the wheel but copying what others that have excellence in that arena are doing and saying. When you find your mentor, ask them lots of questions to find out the strategies they use for success in their area of expertise. An example of questions you might ask someone that has optimum health and vitality might be:

1. Describe for me your average week.
2. How many times per day do you eat?
3. How often do you exercise?
4. What is your strategy when you go out socially for dinner?
5. What kind of exercise do you do?
6. How do you monitor your progress?
7. What are the three key things I must know about health and vitality?
8. What kind of foods do you eat most?

9. How big are your portions?
10. What happens if you skip your exercise one day?
11. How do you motivate yourself?
12. What kind of things do you say to yourself prior to exercise if you don't feel like it?
13. What keeps you going when the going gets tough?

The questions are endless. Your list may be similar or completely different depending on what you find challenging in those areas. My suggestion to you would be to write a list out before seeing this person and then dissect exactly how they do what they do best. You might like to record it like in an interview if you only get access to this person once or perhaps ask them to be your mentor and meet with them regularly to establish and maintain the modelling of their behaviour and strategies.

Qualities to look for in a *personal mentor/coach*:

- They are trustworthy, reliable, and dependable
- Have expertise gained from experience
- Are non-judgemental
- Are positive, fun, and enjoyable to be around
- Don't give up easily
- Will be honest with you and get tough with you if you need it
- Will forgive your failures and encourage you to stick to it despite them
- You feel comfortable sharing your feelings and thoughts with
- You are confident they can help you
- Are as committed to a healthy lifestyle as you are
- Genuinely care about your health and happiness and are happy to help

It's in the actions and the doing that you create your future and change happens.

The importance of *action* and *doing* cannot be underestimated or omitted in the pursuit of any goal or desired outcome. If you bought this book in the hope that just by reading it, it will turn you into a slimmer person, then you are fooling yourself. There is a system to be followed, and the purpose of the three tasks at the end of each chapter is to get you into the habit of doing the do's. It's only in doing the do's that the being comes.

Big goals are meant to be hard to achieve and require determination and staying power.

21 Questions to Move You Towards the Change You Want

I have put together this list of questions for you to really dig deep into the reasons you want to create a change in your weight. They can be used for any area that you want a change in, so please feel free to revisit them many times over when you feel stuck. You will notice that they are created to leverage as much pain and pleasure to move you to action towards your change.

Answer the Following Questions in Order

(Don't read through all of them, just do one at a time and have at least three answers per question, trust what comes up, and write it down.)
Think about the area you want to change (which in your case has been to lose your weight and be healthier).

1. What is this choice costing you right now?
2. What would be the consequence of having this behaviour?
3. What would happen if you kept going down this path?
4. What's the benefit of this choice or staying as you are? If you are tempted to say, 'Nothing', I would respond 'There is a benefit or you wouldn't do it. On some level, this is working for you. We all do what works on some level!'
5. How is that working for you? It is working for you because you are doing it?
6. What is staying the same give you that acting wouldn't?
7. What do you like about this choice?
8. What do you like about procrastination? If you say, 'Nothing', my response to you would be, 'Nothing. Yet you do it so well.'
9. What are you choosing to tolerate?
10. What will it cost you in two, five, ten years?
11. What is it costing those around you?
12. What don't you have because of this?
13. What are you missing out on?
14. If you were able to do this differently, how would that be?
15. If you were to think about it, how could it be?

16. What is your compelling reason for changing this right now?
17. What would be the downside in changing this?
18. What's the biggest bonus or secret bonus in changing this?
19. What will changing this give you or allow you to do?
20. What will you no longer be tolerating? 'Everything' is not an answer. *Be specific.*
21. What will other people and you notice even more?

So how did you go? Your commitment to this exercise will also reflect the commitment you have towards your desired outcome in weight loss.

Procrastination

I like to call this horrible word self-sabotage. So why do we all indulge in procrastination? Is it to keep safe, certain, and stay in the comfort zone? We think that's the reason, and in reality, we are doing nothing more but avoiding the inevitable pain that could be eliminated if we only took action earlier.

When I talk about procrastination with my clients, they often focus on being perfectionists and are constantly looping without ever finishing anything.

Perfection Is a Lack of Standards!

Change does not come about from procrastinating. Waiting for the right moment to start and make a decision on the way forward is pointless and a waste of time. There are three keys if you want to create a change in your life and those are:

- Focus on what you want (your vision)
- Take massive action (it's in the action that change happens)
- Have behavioural flexibility

Behavioural flexibility

This is the ability to adjust your behaviour if you are not getting the results you are after. For example, if a certain diet or exercise regime is not working out for you, then your ability to change to something different will give you more choice and leverage in creating the change you are after.

Top 3 tasks to be completed from this chapter:

1. Complete the twenty-one questions in this chapter for an area in your life you are stuck in. (These apply to any area, not just weight loss.)
2. Seek out a coaching mentor that you can try out and experience a coaching session. There are many coaches out there that will offer your first session as a complimentary one. You will walk away with a few insights and see how coaching can help you reach your goals faster.
3. Reward yourself for a day—just you! If you have been following the tasks set so far, you absolutely deserve it.

PART 2

CREATING YOUR ULTIMATE LIFESTYLE

Chapter 8

The Ultimate Secret to Outstanding Relationships

> When you struggle with your partner, you are struggling with yourself. Every fault you see in them touches a denied weakness in yourself.
>
> (Deepak Chopra)

Do you ever wonder why some couples are so happy and connected to one another and your relationship is lacking the spark and energy that it used to have in the early days? Why do so many marriages end in divorce? And why do more and more women remain single for such a long time in life? All of these questions will be answered in this transformational chapter that will allow you to bring about awareness in your life and ensure a loving and successful relationship with your partner.

The first thing I would like to explore with you is the concept of masculine and feminine energies that exist in all of us and how this has been thrown off balance by the women's revolution and subsequent career choices and roles of women within today's society.

Nowadays, it is unusual for a woman to be staying at home and just looking after the household. This is especially evident in women that have not had children yet. Even when they do have children, it is hard to find a mum that stays at home to raise her children. They often return to work rapidly after having their babies, if not full-time, definitely part-time, to sustain the lifestyle the family enjoyed prior to having children. For some, it may be necessary to have both parents working full-time because the income from one is not enough to survive.

In the external world, women have their feminine energy, however, the demands of today's career woman are that of masculine energy. When the woman is at home, she is masculine and the man is feminine. Now you may ask, 'How is that so?' Women are usually the decision makers about the household. It is their territory, and anything to do with the house is their decision. Just think, if you are a woman, when was the last time you let any item enter your home without your final approval? So by needing to be masculine in the external world and with her usual role in the home world, *today's woman hardly ever gets the chance to experience the feminine side of her which craves to feel safe and protected.*

On the flip side, men have that balance, where they are in their masculine role in the external world and resolve to the feminine energy when at home. They usually have a garden to nurture and feel protected and safe by the woman making all the decisions around the household. Men like to feel successful and appreciated. The paradox here is this: How can he feel successful if he is with another bull? This is where a lot of men have turned into SNAGs (sensitive new age guys), but it is not what women are truly after. They want protection and safety from their man, and the moment they feel the need to make the money, they don't feel safe.

The issue around who makes more money is also one that a lot of men struggle with nowadays. This affects their confidence, self-esteem, and need to feel appreciated. Ladies, always remember and practice this if you are making more than your man: *as long as your man brings home the bread (literally), you can earn as much as you like.*

The Seasons of a Relationship

We all know that all relationships go through a cycle and that as time passes, we grow together and experience different challenges, successes, and frustrations with one another. If you gain an understanding about this, then it will result in your truly loving the different seasons and knowing where you are at with your partner at a certain point in the future. So let's start . . .

Spring

Love is in the air. You have probably just met someone new and are in lust with the idea of them. There are absolutely no faults you can find with them, and everything they say and do is just dreamy. This season in a relationship usually lasts around ninety days or a bit longer if you are not seeing each other too often.

During spring, both parties tend to be doing all sorts of new stuff together. Activities they like or don't like are not an issue because all they are interested in is being together. All love strategies are played out by lots of looking, talking, listening, and touching. Everything is magical and feels like it will last forever.

Summer

Summer lasts somewhere between six and eighteen months. This is the stage that you tend to stop doing things you didn't like before but you did them to make your partner happy. It is during this season that couples make a decision on moving in together. They spend quality time together, have fun, and settle into routines, and this is when the real testing starts to occur. I will explain the test women would put their men through a bit later in the chapter.

Independence is attractive to both sexes. Men may also start to think they don't have to woo the woman anymore at this time. They enter her tree (in this case, the house), and what women actually need is to continue to be chased. In order for this to occur, they must continue to look nice for their man even when at home and for their dates, not just for their girlfriends. Women want to have a king. To allow for this, men want their freedom to be able to do masculine stuff like playing sports. When men are really happy, they are energised and when they are not, they shut down. Watching and playing sports are two very different activities. Let your man go out and play, and you will have your king.

Going to pubs and clubs are masculine activities. Going for lunch, shopping, and spas are feminine activities. A man may feel threatened if you go out to pubs and clubs with your girlfriends looking nice and done up, because he doesn't want to share you with other men. If you like those types of activities, do them with your man and save the feminine activities when catching up with your girlfriends.

Autumn

This is where a decision is made if a relationship will continue or if a break up is imminent. This season is for reaping. The couple starts to question, 'Is this all there is?' It is very important at this stage for couples to give birth to something new and continue to do so every two years in their relationship going forward. This may be by having a child, starting a business or a project, going on a big adventure, or taking up a hobby they can both nurture and enjoy.

Imagine having something new every couple of years to keep the excitement alive and create growth for both of you as time passes.

Winter

When we make it to winter, the roots have gotten deeper, and it is a time of reflection. Couples may be in a positive or negative place in this season. As winter passes, we enter spring once again. This time, spring may not be the brand new relationship, but the education begins once again and new seeds are planted to nurture and grow.

The Test

Early in a relationship, a woman begins testing her man. Men have to pass the test, otherwise the relationship will not continue as far as the woman is concerned. You may be wondering what this test is? It is the test to see if the man will stand by her no matter what, take care of her, and give her the fairytale that she is after. Usually a woman will test the man early in the relationship, but she can test him again and again if she feels tired or overwhelmed because he hasn't done something for her that she needs.

Women need to empty. Only by emptying do they come to their own solutions and feel much better and less overwhelmed. During the test, a woman would be very upset, feeling like everything is her responsibility, blaming, pointing fingers at the man, and projecting a lot of anger and frustration. There may be other emotions going on all at the same time. It has all come about due to her over-functioning in life.

So what does a man do in this circumstance? Well, I will first tell you what not to do and then the correct response.

Don't:
1. Console her—this shows that she is weak.
2. Shrug your shoulders
3. Offer solutions and interrupt her

4. Get defensive
5. Blame her back
6. Joke or laugh
7. Fidget and hold your arms in a defensive stance
8. Talk back to prove a point
9. Let her walk/run out without chasing after her
10. Act or respond defeated
11. Fail the test, otherwise you may be compromising the relationship

Do:
1. Stand calmly in a neutral posture
2. Arms down palms pointing away from her
3. Keep asking 'What else?' or 'How else are you feeling?' until she empties
4. Keep listening
5. Chase after her if she runs away
6. Once finished, grab her face and say, 'I am here for you, I'll take care of you, (and the children if it applies) and I love you.'
7. Finish off with a big love hug (All of the above are using his feminine energy with a warrior)

Romance—Intimacy—Sex—who is responsible for what?

For a loving, fulfilling, and long-term successful relationship, there needs to be a balance in what each person does. When the responsibilities in all of this are understood by both sides, you will wonder how you ever did it any other way.

Romance—is the responsibility of the man. Booking restaurants, weekends away, organising romantic set-ups, the whole lot!

Intimacy—is also the responsibility of the man. Kissing, hugging, and holding hands are to be instigated by the man.

Sex—when the prior two are fulfilled, the woman will be ready and more than willing to instigate the sex and make the man feel appreciated and needed.

This is where I many of my clients get a bit of a shock (especially the men). But it is very simple, and it makes a lot of sense. Women take a lot longer to get the desire to want to be intimate with their partner, whereas a man can turn it on at the drop of a hat. That is why wooing should be a lifelong act by the man towards the woman. She will feel part of that fairytale and have her king by her side.

Monogamous relationships are the most powerful!

The Two Key Reasons Why Relationships/Marriages Fail

When I learnt about these two reasons, it became very clear to me where I had gone wrong in the past and how I could make sure my future was going to have my partner by my side right to the end. Now that I know this, I often speak to others about it and educate my clients so that they have successful relationships that are more loving and fulfilling going forward.

- **Negative anchoring**

This one is huge. I will first explain what anchoring is and how it can trigger different states or memories at the press of a button. Anchoring is a process whereby a stimulus may be applied (by touching, hearing, smelling, tasting, or seeing), and it triggers a specific response that has been anchored. An example might be hearing a song from your childhood that reminds you of a particular event, the smell of your grandmother's cooking that, when triggered, takes you back in time to remember her and what you did together.

Hearing a tuning fork ring was the stimulus Pavlov anchored in his experiment with the dogs. He would ring the fork and give the dogs some food. Then he would do it again and again until the time when he did, the dogs started to salivate even though there was no food coming. They were conditioned by Pavlov to have this response, and the anchor was the sound of the tuning fork.

So how does anchoring affect our relationships? When we are speaking to our partner, it is important to understand anchoring. In the beginning of a relationship, all anchoring is positive and loving, so that each time you see your partner, they are very appealing and you feel lots of love and affection towards them.

As time passes, arguments, fighting, and anger are situations and emotions that are expressed between partners. If you continue to look at each other when expressing negative feelings, disappointment, or frustration, the process

"However good or bad you feel about your relationship, the person you are with at this moment is the "right" person, because he or she is the mirror of who you are inside."
                              Deepak Chopra

of negative anchoring starts to occur until one day, the negative anchors have been stacked so high that you feel like you don't love your partner anymore and the sight of him/her is bringing up feelings of dislike and unease. It is at this time that people either separate or grow apart or stay in the relationship for reasons other than love. You may be wondering at this stage if you can reverse this or how do you go about avoiding it from now on.

The Solution ...

Yes, you can reverse it and avoid it! It is very simple and easy. It will require you building a muscle of awareness and new habits to implement going forward in your relationship. The new habit involves you remembering that when you are having serious discussions and arguments, never look at your partner directly. Sit facing away from each other and have these discussions away from the bedroom and bathroom. After all, the last place you want to anchor negative feelings is the places where you consummate your love. Instead, have the discussion in other parts of your home or, even better, step outside, go for a walk, and look straight ahead as you are talking about your challenges and frustrations.

These suggestions are simple, but they do require discipline and the ability to remember at times of frustration to not revert back to your old ways. When you begin with these techniques, it will seem unusual, especially if you are used to a completely different way of resolving issues in your relationship. With time and being persistent, you will create unconscious competence around this. You will have a renewed relationship, where your partner and you will grow in love and appreciation for one another once again.

- **Unfulfilled Love Strategies**

Every single person experiences deep love in a different way. What this means is that people either feel loved by seeing, talking, hearing, or touching. We all have a preferred representational system that creates that deep love connection within us. For example:

Visual love is felt by seeing your partner look nice and really appreciating all the effort they go through to keep up their appearance for you. When you are in surroundings that are visually appealing to you, this enhances your experience of deep love with your partner.

Auditory love is when you experience love by hearing loving words, pet names, and feelings being expressed verbally to you. An auditory person would love soft music and sweet nothings whispered to them from their partner.

Kinaesthetic love is when you experience love by being touched or touching your partner. Cuddling, kissing, and physical touch are most important for you to feel the deep love connection. The seeing and hearing parts may not be important at all in how you experience love.

Auditory digital love or talking is when you experience love by being listened to when talking about what is going on inside (your self-talk). The conversation can be about anything, not just loving feelings. When you feel listened to about your concerns and way forward, you feel like you have shared and your partner loves you by being your sounding board.

Now that you understand the distinction between the four ways we all experience deep love, you may be wondering what it has to do with how relationships fail because of this. Well, the fact is that when a relationship starts out, both parties are wooing each other in any way they can think of. Just think back to the beginning of one of your relationships.

There is a lot of touching, kissing, buying each other presents, giving each other compliments, dressing up and looking nice for one another, and definitely a lot of talking and listening from both parties. It's fair to say that all of the love strategies are being fulfilled for each person, and that is why we call this the honeymoon period.

As time passes and we enter the summer stage of the relationship, we tend to revert back to what our love strategy is and do that only. In most cases, couples' love strategies will differ from one another. The trick and solution to this is to work out what your love strategy is and that of your partner's so you can start fulfilling theirs rather than just doing yours.

There are two ways to figure out what a person's deep love strategy is. One is by asking them the question: 'Can you remember a specific time when you felt totally loved? What was happening exactly? Was it something you were hearing, feeling, or seeing?' Get the person to describe to you the situation and work out exactly what was going on that triggered the love inside of them.

The second way to find out someone's love strategy is to notice what they stop doing when they get angry with you. You can do this for yourself by thinking back to a time you got upset with your partner: What is it that you stopped doing to punish them? The thing that you stopped doing is your deep love strategy, because that is exactly what you like being done to you when you want to be loved.

We love people in the way we would like to be loved. This is where relationships break down and come to a halt. We only end up fulfilling our own love strategy, which is not the way our partner feels deep love and connection. They don't get their love strategy met, and they don't feel loved throughout the relationship.

The Solution . . .

Spend some time working out what yours and your partner's deep love strategy is. If you are not sure how to do that, seek out a relationship coach that can help you through the process. The next thing is start loving them in the way they feel deep love. So if they like hearing how much you love them, give them just that—lots of verbally expressed love. If you like being touched as a way of feeling loved, then share this with your partner so that he/she starts doing more of that to make you feel the deep love connection.

Once again, it does take some time to build a muscle around this because it is different, new, and unfamiliar to most people. If the desire is there to build a truly fulfilling love and connection with your partner, then you will follow up and do the above mentioned suggestions.

Find Your Model of Excellence for Relationships

We have spoken quite in depth about the necessity to find mentors and models that are getting the results you are after. Every mentor that you find out there may have excellence in a particular area of life that is important for you to excel at. I recently found my model of excellence in relationships and asked her lots of questions about how she got to have such a satisfying, fun, and loving relationship. What is it that keeps the spark going for her and her husband? Finding this mentor was very hard, because so far in life, I have been surrounded by failed relationships, marriages, and models of how not to be.

I believe it is important to share her answers with you since you also may be in a similar situation as I was, struggling to find my model of excellence. Here is a breakdown of some of her responses regarding her relationship:

She has a ten-page ideal partner list that is very specific. She also keeps adding to this list from time to time and sees her wishes come to reality in most cases. She knows what she wants and goes after it. Project out there what you want to attract in your life. She doesn't share her list with her partner, but they do share their vision together.

- She believes that if you are attracted to your partner, it means you are attracted to yourself.
- She also found other couples that were extremely happy and asked them how they did what they did.
- She knew the importance of nurturing something outside the relationship, but the marriage always remained as the number one priority.
- Date night once a week.
- Romantic getaways once a quarter.
- They are best friends as well as lovers.
- They are never apart longer than two to three nights at a time.
- They have a great sex life, often experiment with sex toys, watching videos and constantly educating themselves around the subject of sex to improve their sex life. They believe sex gets better as you get older.
- They have never lived apart. They believe it is the worst thing for relationships.
- They have sex two to five times per week and three times per day if they are away
- They engage in lots of kissing every single day. Wet kisses especially!
- They shower together often and have a double shower for this purpose.
- They make an effort to dress up sexy for one another and look feminine or masculine for one another.
- Their date nights are usually not restaurants but fun activities and experiences where they can laugh and be adventurous.

Quality time together in the relationship builds rapport. You will grow a million times faster with your partner than if you were on your own. The above list may seem a bit unrealistic to a lot of people, but you can take what you want out of it. Even by implementing a few strategies of the model of excellence, you will start seeing a drastic improvement in the quality of your relationship.

In the final section of this chapter, I would like to spend some time painting a picture for you of how men and women differ in their needs and wants and how you can overcome and adjust your behaviour to have an outstanding relationship with your partner.

30 Ways to Make Your Partner Happy

	Women	Men
1	Want to be listened to without offering solutions	Want to be told they have been helpful after listening
2	Like to be acknowledged first as soon as you get home	Love coming home to a happy woman—makes them feel successful
3	Expect men to know when they need support	Ask for support when they need it
4	Need respect to feel loved	Need appreciation to feel loved
5	Find it difficult to support men when they don't talk	Find it difficult to support women when they do talk
6	Use words to share emotions	Use words to share information
7	Needs someone to listen to her feelings	Needs to be trusted
8	Use 'always' and 'never' when feeling insecure	Take generalisations literally and get defensive
9	Feel unloved without nurturing communication	Must learn the skill of listening
10	Value love, communication, beauty, and relationships	Value admiration, appreciation, recognition, and trust
11	Sense of self is defined by her feelings and quality of her relationships	Sense of self is defined through the ability to achieve results
12	Like to receive gifts as a surprise not just special occasions	Want to give more when they are not expected to
13	Like to have their feeling validated when they are upset	Like to be told you love them when they are upset
14	Symptoms of stress: overreaction, feeling overwhelmed, and exhaustion	Symptoms of stress: withdrawal, grumbling, and shutting down
15	Deepest fear: being abandoned	Deepest fear: that he is incompetent
16	Like lots of hugs	Like a massage

	Women	Men
17	Greatest challenge: to let go off resentment and find forgiveness	Greatest challenge: to take responsibility for his contribution to a problem
18	Like being called to be told they are loved	Like to find love notes only they can see
19	Don't like being judged for needing reassurance	Don't like to be judged for needing to withdraw
20	Like for men to be on their side when they are upset with someone	Like to be told: 'It's not your fault'
21	Argue for the right to be upset	Argue for the right to be free
22	Need to receive caring, understanding, and reassurance	Need to receive trust, acceptance, and appreciation
23	Like it when men fix something around the house	Like to be thanked for the little things they do.
24	Want to be listened to patiently not passively	Want to be asked to do things in a loving way
25	Communicate to make a point, discover more, and experience intimacy	Communicate to make a point or solve a problem
26	The more she feels the right to be upset, the less upset she will be	Talk about their problems so they can find a solution
27	Get in touch with emotions by talking	Get in touch with their feelings by listening to other people's problems
28	Don't appreciate being told how to change their feelings	Don't like being told what to do
29	Like to be asked specific questions about their day	Like to be given space to recover from the stress of their day
30	Will close up when a man dumps anger on them	His self-esteem is not based on being sensitive to others' feelings

Top 3 Tasks to Be Completed from This Chapter:

1. Get your partner to read this chapter with you and have a discussion about it together.
2. Pick three different strategies that you will focus on over the next week and then review and reset new ones for the following week.
3. Work out each other's deep love strategy and start fulfilling your partner's.

Chapter 9

The Ultimate Secret to Fantastic Finances

Investing is simple, but not easy.
(Warren Buffet)

Are you sick of living your life on credit? Would you like to have a lump sum of money you can fall back on if unforeseen circumstances strike? How about the ability to generate passive income so that you can choose how you live your life and where and with whom you spend the most precious commodity—time?

There are only two excuses or reasons why people fail to take action on their dreams so they can live their ideal life. Not enough time or not enough money. These two key areas in our lives limit us and our potential, instilling fear that if we were to take a risk, the chances are we would fail. The focus generally goes to the negative and undesirable outcome, which is what becomes reality. Earlier we spoke about finding more time in your life to be able to achieve your goals. In this chapter, I would like to give you the tools and strategies to get your finances back on track and design a life that is heading towards you having your perfect, ideal, average day.

The perfect, ideal, average day is one that is just that—average! You are not on holiday or doing things that are unusual. It is simply how you would spend your time if you had the choice to do whatever you like. You may decide to start your days late, read, socialise, or go shopping. Whichever way you see it is perfect for you.

Did you know that more than 50 per cent of people have only one month of savings for emergencies in developed countries such as Australia and America? Over 60 per cent also live pay check to pay check, which is a statistic

Family budgets

I get asked 'What for?' It is staggering to know that people don't have a concept of what is going in, coming out, and whether they can afford the lifestyle they are living. This is very scary and unfortunate, especially when these individuals start having children and the cost of living jumps up to a new level with often less income and higher expenditure.

I would like to share with you some of the secrets to improve your finances and start generating wealth that will see you live out your life in luxury rather than in lack. One other famous statistic to become familiar with is:

By the time people reach retirement age:
1-2 per cent are wealthy
75 per cent are on welfare
23 per cent are dead

Which statistic would you like to belong to when you retire?

Our education about finances starts very early in life. Think about who you had as a role model around you growing up. Were they good with money or just made ends meet at the end of each pay cycle? Our beliefs about how we manage money and, more importantly, how we make it are set well before we turn seven years of age. I will discuss the period of zero to seven in the following chapter when we look at parenting.

It is very important to know where what you believe about money and finances comes from and, if necessary, to start creating new beliefs that will serve you going forward.

Beliefs Creation—My Story

At this stage, I would like to illustrate how beliefs around money are created by sharing my story in this particular area. I grew up in Macedonia mostly around female role models belonging to the middle class there. My main role models were my mum and auntie (or the way I like to call them—

my two mums). My mum separated from my dad before I was three years old, and I was surrounded by strong independent women that looked after themselves and were the breadwinners for the family. These two women can also be called my Rich Mum and Poor Mum, just like Robert Kiyosaki has described his two dads that he had as role models in his now famous book *Rich Dad Poor Dad*.

My Rich Mum, my auntie, was a banker, and I would often visit her at work and learn about the ways banks operate. I held an account from a very young age, where my savings would go in. My auntie always got the things she wanted and planned for the future well ahead of time. One thing I haven't mentioned is that she is disabled (she has had polio since she was two) and has always worked twice as hard as her siblings to get to where she is today. She is determined and very clever as to the decisions she has made to invest her money. When her bank went under, she could not find a job anywhere else. The economic state of the country was on a downslide, and jobs were rare for fully fit individuals, let alone someone that had a disability.

She invested the money she had earned and saved over the years in a retail store and a couple of one-bedroom apartments. This is her livelihood today. The rental income (passive income) from these three holdings (two businesses and a retail store) is supporting her lifestyle, and she is able to independently look after herself without any financial assistance from anyone else. She pays her bills on time, goes on holidays, and drives new cars. She has been living her ideal, average perfect day for years now. In fact, it has been over fifteen years since her bank was closed and she hasn't worked a day.

The beliefs that I have created by watching her as a child are that you have to save up and budget your money if you want to have comfort and buy what you desire. I know planning for the distant future is a must if you want to have a fun retirement where you live out your days exploring and enjoying time with your family. You have to work towards creating passive income from various avenues that I will reveal later on.

So what about my Poor Mum? This is my real mum. She is also good with money and savings, but is nearing her retirement without an ounce of passive income and most likely will end up on welfare. I must say there are great traits that I have from her like determination, being a hard worker, and the ability to fit into surroundings quickly and easily, not finances or money. I watched my mum work three jobs while I was very young. She went to her full-time job from seven to three as a draftsman, put together crosswords for the paper in the afternoons, and then she would go and be a bingo speaker at nights. It felt like she was doing this for a very long time.

The beliefs I created as a result of this were: it's hard to make money, you have to work many hours to live a comfortable lifestyle, and you must always have back-up in case of emergencies. My mum has always had good back-up, but this is only for the short term. If she was to stop working today, in a few short months, her funds would run out, since they are not passive and reoccurring, and she would have to sell her home to support herself further. It would be that or live on a tiny welfare cheque with just the minimal staples to support herself.

So where does that leave me today? I am great with money and keeping debt to a bare minimum or none (aside from the mortgage). I am able to enjoy a couple of holidays per year with my family because I am a great saver. I am working on my ventures to create passive income for the future and modelling people well ahead in the money game for excellence and results I haven't witnessed around me yet. My mindset has grown to a level that I will invest in my education to learn new tools and strategies that will get me ahead in my finances so that I can reach my ideal, average perfect day sooner and enjoy the things I love most—spending time with my family and travelling the world.

Where to start...

Financial freedom and independence is definitely a journey and not a destination. It takes time to master this skill and turn it into reality. Just like a muscle needs working out to build up and be strong, so does your financial IQ. I would start with your education. Invest a small amount of money purchasing a few books from a book store around simple financial planning, budgets, and wealth creation. You can also do this online by buying some e-books or doing an online course. The information age has brought about lots of valuable and practical tools that anyone can implement in their lives. The two books that truly made an impact on me and helped me understand wealth creation and investments were:

Rich Dad Poor Dad by Robert Kiyosaki (I subsequently read all of the spin-offs from that book) and *You Were Born Rich* by Bob Proctor. *Think and Grow Rich* by Napoleon Hill is also a fantastic resource on mindset and how abundant people have brought about wealth into their lives.

It is only by investing in our education that we will grow and be open to new opportunities and choices. We don't know what we don't know. That's why the first secret to fantastic finances is to invest in your education and put into action the new things you learn so you can test and measure what is a perfect fit for you.

Getting Rid of Debt

How much debt do you have? What does your income and expenditure look like? Robert Kiyosaki often states in his books that a person is capable of getting rid of all their debt in seven years or less. Start today! Spend less than what you earn and get out of the red forever. Learn how to create a simple home budget that you will stick to no matter what. I have been creating my own budgets since I got my first job. This is how I've been able to get the things I want, travel to all the countries I have visited, and purchase the homes and cars we own today.

To create your own individual or family budget, I have enclosed a template in Appendix E that you can follow, add, and remove items as you need to. Something as simple as this will give you a snapshot of what is going in and coming out throughout the year.

If you find out there is more coming out than going in, then this is a red flag that you need to re-evaluate where your money is going and cut down on the spending, if you don't want to get into even more debt. I would suggest re-evaluating your budget to the point that what you spend is less than what you earn, so that you can use the residual money to start paying off your debt. In the beginning, it will seem very difficult and unusual to go without all of the luxuries you have grown accustomed to. Within a few short weeks, the new habits of spending will become more concrete, and you won't be bothered as much about the old stuff.

If your income and expenses are just even, once again have a look at where you can cut down to minimise and eliminate all debt so that you can start looking at investing your extra money into one of the four main money-making vehicles discussed later.

THE 7 ULTIMATE SECRETS TO WEIGHT LOSS

Finally, if your expenses are less than your income, then it is time to create some new goals and begin work on wealth creation so long as all debt is paid off and your living expenses are easily covered. So how do you split your income? Here is a suggestion that you may want to consider:

- You pay yourself first by taking out 10 per cent of your income.
- Have a savings account where you save another 10 per cent of your income.
- Use 70 per cent of your income for your living expenses.
- Have a debt repayment programme that may need to come into play for emergencies. This should be around 5-10 per cent of your income.

Top 20 tips on how you can save some money and repay debt instead

1. Take your lunch to work and make lunches for the whole family. This one is a very big saver, and you get to be healthier along the way, avoiding junk food and having variety from your own fridge.
2. Invite friends over instead of going out. Once again, you can choose to cook healthy, well-balanced meals, and you can take turns at hosting the dinner parties. This cuts down the cost of socialising and entertainment significantly, and you can have all your kids together to play. This way, you end up saving money on babysitting as well.
3. Evaluate any items on your budget that you might not need and cancel them. This might be some extra channels on your pay TV package, reduction of your mobile phone plan, or cancellation of any memberships you may not be using all that often anymore.
4. Reduce your TV-watching hours. It will save on electricity, but the big bucks come from you being less exposed to guilt-inducing ads, and it gives you more time to focus on other things. This may be more quality time with your family, having a new hobby, or working on your wealth creation by educating yourself in those areas. TV is a very negative medium that induces trance and anchors undesirable states in us.
5. Have a thirty-day rule. This is when you are tempted to make a purchase while out or even on the Internet. You wait thirty days to see if you still want it, and quite often, you will notice that the urge has passed. You can keep a list of this. However, it's better keeping it in your head, which would mean unimportant items get

forgotten anyway well before the thirty days are up.

6. Don't spend too much money entertaining your children, especially young ones that find almost anything fascinating. You can create a game out of anything around the house. Remember, your children want your time, not your stuff. This way, you will find more money in your pocket and more joy in your heart.
7. Drink lots of water. Before you have a meal, have a glass of water. This will fill you up more, make your food digest a lot better, and you will save lots on your food bill by having smaller portions. You will also find yourself feeling better because you will be properly hydrated.
8. Give up expensive habits such as cigarettes, alcohol, and drugs. Need I say more?
9. Make big batches of casserole when you are cooking it so that you can freeze it and have it on nights you find yourself busy and tempted to spend money on takeaway. Think of the health benefits and money saved when you do this.
10. De-clutter your home and make some money selling the stuff you want to get rid of either on eBay or by having a garage sale at home. You will feel a lot more organised and allow for other great things to come into your life.
11. Don't go to stores and shopping centres for entertainment. The temptations are too large to be around places you can spend money. Instead, go to parks, sporting venues, friend's places, the beach, or even entertain yourself at home with a new hobby or playing a game with the family.
12. Swap babysitting with neighbours. This will eliminate the need to pay for babysitters, and your children will get to know each other more and have more company around.
13. Go through all of your clothes every six months. You will be amazed at the items you will discover that have been sitting at the back of your wardrobe, and you will feel like you have new clothes to wear. If some items you find are totally not your style anymore, sell them on eBay and make some cash that you can spend on new items.
14. Check out what your local community board has on offer. Often you will find social groups you can join for free, nice parks, free tennis courts, basketball courts, trails, and other outdoor activities.
15. Don't speed or break any other road rules. Firstly, you will save on fuel consumption, but mostly, you will be safer, save on fines, convictions, and endangering other people's lives.

"Risk comes from not knowing what you're doing."
Warren Buffet

16. Don't overspend on hygiene products. You only need one shampoo, conditioner, toothpaste, or deodorant. Stacking your bathroom cupboards, drawers, and shower with ten different choices is a waste of money and creates a lot of clutter. The products also have an expiry date, so after six to twelve months of opening, their active ingredients won't be as effective.
17. Cut down on holiday spending. Instead of taking expensive holidays overseas, hire a camper van and see your beautiful country. After all, you want quality time with your family, and travelling from place to place can be exciting and very adventurous for kids.
18. Buy your staple items for the house in bulk. This cuts down the cost per usage significantly, and in the long term, it will save you a bundle of money.
19. Don't beat yourself up over a mistake. If you have made ten good choices and one that is not, it's OK as long as you realise and take on the feedback that it was a mistake and you will know better next time.
20. Never give up! Keep educating yourself and looking for other solutions if your problem of debt is not going away.

Wealth Creation Vehicles

Most of today's population is in what we call the rat race. What this means is that if people in the rat race stopped going to work, they would not be able to support themselves and their families. The amount of time it would take to spend their entire back-up and savings is not very long—about a month at best as we had learnt earlier! It's a scary thought knowing that you have to work your whole life to be able to survive, and then when you stop, you get to go on a tiny pension that may or may not enable you to just scrape by. Do you want a life like that? Or do you want to be able to decide how and with whom you spend your time?

I am sure most of you would choose the second option. I know I am working towards exiting the rat race and entering the fast track so that I can have more choices and opportunities to be able to help others do the same. There are four main avenues through which you can do this. They are:
- Business
- Internet
- Shares
- Property

Some choose to master just one, and others get involved in two, three, or all four ways of leveraging their time and income to create the ideal lifestyle on the fast track. Let's now spend some time discussing these briefly so that I can paint you a picture of how they work and eventually give you the freedom and opportunity to decide what you do for the rest of your life.

Business

Starting your own business can be very exiting and rewarding. You can choose what you are passionate about and turn it into a profit-making machine. Just imagine doing something you absolutely love and getting paid for it. Will it feel like work? Not in the slightest.

Going into business has lots of benefits and just as many drawbacks that can put you off or discourage you. At times, you may want to quit and go back to your usual occupation—back into the rat race. The key is to decide that it's going to work and keep yourself centred and focused on the end in mind. In my experience of starting my own business, these are some of the benefits and drawbacks I found:

Benefits of having your own business:

- flexibility and choice of who you work with and what happens in the business
- living and working with your passion
- helping others is extremely rewarding
- creating and nurturing something from scratch
- complete control and decision-making power over the business
- potential to grow the business to a company or franchise, put it up on the stock exchange, and eventually sell it for a big profit

Drawbacks of having your own business:

- Start up costs can be large
- Marketing the business in the beginning is costly
- You may not have an income or see a profit for a couple of years. Usually money that comes in will go back into growing the business further

- Income can vary up and down, depending on the current demand for your goods or services
- Building a business from scratch can be time-consuming and challenging if you haven't done it before
- Determination, persistence, and behavioural flexibility are keys to your success

The general pattern of how businesses start out is with a person having an idea and bringing it to life. In the early days, it is just them playing all the roles in the business. They are managing director, manufacturer, marketing expert, sales consultant, technician, and personal assistant. Without them, the business would not exist at all. This is what we call the infancy stage of a business. With time, it is important that the business owner creates systems and procedure manuals for the business so that if anyone else was to come along and do the same job as the business owner, they have the systems documented and are able to follow the exact steps. As this is happening, the owner is able to bring on staff and share with them the systems for their role. This would usually continue until such time that all the roles within the business have been covered and the owner can remove themselves from working 'in' the business to working 'on' the business.

When working 'on' the business, the owner is able to grow the brand by selling it as a franchise (like McDonald's), leverage their time, and get a percentage of the profits from all the franchises. Eventually, a decision can be made to completely sell the brand and business systems to someone for a large sum of money. This would result in the owner being financially free and independent for the rest of their lives. As soon as the owner is able to remove himself from working in the business, his life is on the fast track, and they are reaping all the fruits of their labour.

Examples of some businesses that started of as one and grew to these levels are: McDonald's, KFC (was started when the owner was in his sixties), Boost Juice Bars, Body Shop, Google, Facebook, and others.

The possibilities are endless, and the only thing stopping you from being successful in business is you. If you like the sound of this wealth creation vehicle, make sure you do lots of research and educate yourself around business and marketing so you can fast track and get outstanding results quicker. Invest in mentors that are ahead of you in the game of business and marketing because their advice will be invaluable, and this investment will be returned back to you ten-fold in the future.

Internet

The power of the Internet has brought the whole world to our doorstep. The exposure it allows means that the potential is huge for an Internet-based business. You can easily generate income via the Internet from the comfort of your own home. There are many different types of businesses you can run through the Internet. Here are some examples:

- Membership sites
- Affiliate marketing for Google and other large companies
- Selling a specific product where there is a huge market and a hungry crowd (long sales letter pages for a specific product have been known to generate millions for some people)
- Online store where you outsource everything to others
- Online courses for people to attend

The possibilities are endless. Lots of people turn their eBay accounts into a business where they resell products they shop for at sale times. This type of business can create a lot of passive income for you, or it can replace your nine-to-five job and give you more flexibility around your family and children. The Internet is used to grow any business, and it is the first place people would go to nowadays to do a bit of research on you before coming to do business with you.

The key to successfully use the Internet and, more importantly, start generating income from it is to invest some money into a system that works or learn from the experts that are already getting results in that area. There are numerous books on Internet marketing, writing web copy, and how to start a business online. As always, investing time and money is necessary if you want to leave the rat race once and for all.

Having attended many seminars on wealth creation, I can tell you that the choices and possibilities are endless if you have the staying power and are willing to learn and invest in yourself. There are very successful individuals that can teach you their system for the fraction of the cost that will take you to your desired results. The one thing you must possess is patience and willingness to learn and follow a system.

Shares

There are a lot of people that have shares; in fact, your superannuation is invested in all sorts of shares. This wealth creation vehicle can be very lucrative and easy to do once you know what you are doing. For most people that are speculators of the market, it's a form of gambling that can have adverse effects on their financial security. A person that is a knowledgeable investor in shares will be able to make money in the market whether it is going up or going down. It takes a lot of practice and study of a particular area you choose to invest in when it comes to shares. The different types of shares that you can invest in include:

- growth companies
- stock
- commodities
- currency exchange
- renting shares for a profit

Some of the above will give you ongoing dividends that will be passive income for you, and others will be a one-off profit that you will acquire via buying or selling the shares. There is a lot of psychology involved in the whole process of shares, and that's something you learn and get thoughts on by experts in the field. At times, there is need to be patient and not jump the gun, and at other times, a lot more might be happening because it may be an ideal time to take action on certain deals.

People start off with this wealth creation vehicle usually as a bonus to their job until such time that their income is replaced and they can run their portfolio full-time from home.

Like with the Internet, attend a few seminars where the experts will present to you how they do what they do so successfully around the different options when investing in shares. Once you find a system and type of shares you may be interested to invest in, purchase the education and tools you will need to start with this. Set aside time each day that you will devote in building your education and muscle to get really good at it.

Property

Investing in property is huge, most common amongst people and very lucrative. A lot of people have two to three properties throughout their lifetime. The way you create wealth from property can vary. As one of the four wealth creation vehicles, this one is the safest one, so long as you have patience and hold on to your properties long enough to make a great profit. Statistically, property keeps going up over time. There are a few years that it may stagnate or go backwards, but it has been shown that the momentum is generally forward as long as you wait out the slow periods.

Different people use property for investment in many ways. Some of the ways you can create passive income from property are:

- renting out many positively geared properties
- buying un-renovated properties, doing the renovations, and reselling them straight after for a profit
- negatively gearing a few properties and reselling them after a certain time for a profit
- investing in commercial property

There are lots of do's and don'ts when it comes to investing in property, and you must perform your due diligence when it comes to putting down large amounts of money. Property is one of the most expensive strategies out of the four as a way to ensure your future is comfortable and financially free.

Start small and work up to bigger risks and investments. Get to know the areas that are great to invest in, find out what the legal requirements are, whether you need any permits to extend, redevelop, or renovate. There are many tricks in this type of business that must be learnt and studied if you are to have a successful nest egg in the future.

Where to from here...

To achieve fantastic finances, start with your debt and management style of what is going in and out. Take the actions necessary to be debt-free, and while doing this, start reading up on various ways you can make extra money to start generating passive income. Attend lots of seminars (these are usually free), and find out things you didn't know existed. I certainly did and was amazed at how many different ways there are to get out of the rat race. Once you are ready, have done your research, and found the most attractive form of investment that suits you and your family, put your money where your mouth is, and take the massive action necessary to turn your life around.

With time, you will get better and more knowledgeable as long as the commitment and actions continue to be there. Find the models in that area of investing and copy what they are doing, ask lots of 'how' questions, and create networks with people with the same mindset as you.

Top 3 Tasks to Be Completed from This Chapter:

1. Put together your home budget by using the spreadsheet example provided in Appendix E.
2. Find five areas you will focus on to cut down costs and spending so you can repay debts if you have them.
3. Attend a seminar to learn how others are generating and creating wealth away from the nine-to-five.

Chapter 10

The Ultimate Secret to Successful Parenting

> Don't give your children cash and things, give them goals for wings.

'What have I done?' These were my thoughts as I lay on the king single bed opposite my newborn baby's cot. 'How did I get myself into this and why? Can I send him back? I want my old life back!'

You see, I wasn't your typical clucky thirty-year-old that thought it was time to start having children. In fact, I was quite happy with my job, house, car, and all the travelling and luxuries I had with my husband. I had no desire to start having children. It turned out to be a bit of a project that I was curious about and thought to myself that I have to try this and see what it's like.

Just like any project, I learnt and planned the best ways to fall pregnant and had absolute certainty that if I followed all the rules and the best time to conceive, success would follow. And so it did. Just like I said, planned, and executed, I was pregnant first go and jumped straight into organising the next stage of this process.

There was nothing too hard about being pregnant. I was very active right up to the end. I worked until I was thirty-eight weeks pregnant and often forgot that I was growing another person inside of me. I read books, bought all the gadgets, and prepared everything with the utmost accuracy and precision.

Judd arrived into this world on the eleventh of the eleventh month at 11 a.m. It was cool and different, but love didn't blossom immediately. How do you just become a mum in a split second and have the maternal instinct of love for your baby? I wasn't sure about all that, but I was happy, and everyone around me seemed over the moon.

Breastfeeding was my first challenge. I knew that this was the best for the baby and had heard that it would be great if I was breastfeeding him for the first twelve months. This was a goal I set for myself and Judd. I had to give him the best start in life. And so it began. The torturous breastfeeding sessions that seemed to last forever. It hurt so much that it was causing me to resent my baby. I was in tears in the middle of the night. I asked for help, went to different doctors for advice, read more, and expressed the milk so I wouldn't have to have the baby on my breast while the cracked nipples were working hard to heal themselves.

After many failed attempts to get any relief, I learnt about nipple shields. My lifesavers! No one had even mentioned them until a particular midwife told me about them. I went to the pharmacy immediately, got a pair, and tested it. The pain was reduced by 50 per cent, Judd was getting the breast milk without the need and inconvenience to express, and I was a much happier mum for it. I used the shields for the first three months and often would try without them to see if I could go back to natural feeding. Time and time, I returned to them until one day my nipples had hardened and breastfeeding was a breeze. The rest of the year flew by, and with our travels overseas for three months, the convenience of not carrying any milk around was so simple and easy. I breastfed Judd until the day of his first birthday.

Challenge number 2: Sleepless nights! This one was huge. If you have been reading since the beginning, you would already be familiar with how we overcame this challenge in Chapter 2. The point I would like to illustrate here is that you must attempt lots of different strategies and tactics to find a solution to a challenge you are experiencing. This applies to anything in life. Do something different, if what you are doing is not working. And if it doesn't work—do something else. We know all children are different. That is why doing different things to get the result you are after is essential when it comes to parenting different children. Never ever give up!

There were other challenges along the way: teething, dealing with the huge responsibility of having a child, finding time for the relationship once again, being at home full-time, not feeling like an adult anymore—just to name a few. But by the end of the first year, all of that gets ironed out and mastered.

The love grew and grew, just as he did. I now know what maternal love and connection is. I appreciate my parents that much more, knowing what I know now. It is something that you have to experience and go through to have an understanding of what it is and how it feels.

The next steps...

You have a child, but you don't get given a manual on them. Instead, you do the best you can with the available resources you have and you act as their role model. The 0-7 years is what is known as the imprint period. All our beliefs, values, and opinions about the world around us are formulated during this time. It has also been said that 0-3 is the strongest time frame during which what we do around our children is being taken in and imprinted to formulate the map of reality they will have going through life.

You might ask: 'How can an infant or a toddler create beliefs and decide on what things mean?' There is no *ego* at this stage or what I like to call the 'gatekeeper'. Everything goes straight into the unconscious mind and is considered to be true and fact. It is our responsibility as parents to be aware of this and role model excellence in front of our children. If you want them to grow up strong, confident, and independent, let them help you when they want, encourage them when attempting new things, and spend time with them to show them they are worth it.

The moment you want to be in control is the moment when your child feels they are not good enough to help you. We know that children do not have the analytical ability of adults and their thoughts can be irrational and inaccurate. The imprint occurs when that child tells themselves what something means. There may be moments that you think are irrelevant, but it is those moments that could be the defining moments for your child. They are sponges that see, hear, and feel everything. They may not be able to express themselves, but they know what each look means, the tone of your voice, and how to push your buttons from the time they are toddlers.

Here are a few examples of possible negative imprints:

- Not letting your children help you
- Taking over when they can't do something
- Calling them names that are hurtful or discouraging
- Not spending enough time with them

- Ignoring them when you are busy
- Yelling at them when they have an accident
- Swearing in front of them
- Having fights with your partner in front of them
- Putting them down

All of the above could be creating beliefs that they are not good enough, they can't be independent, they don't matter, that their self-worth is low, that it's normal to be put down and called names, and that relationships between a man and a woman are meant to be the way you model them.

To imprint positive behaviours and self-worth on to your children:

- Encourage them when they are doing new things
- Let them help you whenever they want
- Teach them good language all of the time
- Read lots to them
- Show them lots of love, affection, and attention
- Show them how a loving relationship should be
- Be patient and seek to understand their concerns
- Listen to them
- Spend lots of time with them
- Reward them with praise in front of others and while alone

These behaviours will create resourceful states in your children, and they will know to trust you and confide in you when challenges arise. As they grow and one day leave the nest, they will be able to stand on their own two feet and enjoy fantastic relationships, careers, and be great parents themselves. All of this will happen because you were an outstanding model of excellence for them.

Anchoring Resourceful States

Another great strategy I have implemented with my child is the anchoring of positive and happy states. When Judd is happy, laughing, and excited, I press on his little button nose and anchor those states time and time again. We call this his Happy Button. He often will press my nose to make me happy, and in turn, this changes his state when I press his. This works a treat when he is sad or crying. You can do this on any part of the body, so long as it is not something that would be getting touched all of the time.

Saying 'look up' and pointing up for your distressed child also helps change their state and feelings. When we are feeling great, we tend to look up and access our visual. When we are feeling down, we look down and access our feelings. This works great if your child hits itself and gets hurt. Helping them look up will reduce the focus on the pain and help them recover back to normal much quicker.

Learning Strategies

To give your children the best opportunity in life, teaching them how to learn is crucial. Having the ability to learn easier and quicker will accelerate them through their education. There are four keys to outstanding learning. They are: expanded awareness, the use of colours, the creation of mind maps, and visual recall learning.

Expanded awareness

This is also called the learning state. It enables us to reach deep within our unconscious and find the answers that lie within. This state is useful for anyone, not just children. Teaching your children how to get into expanded awareness will give them the edge over others. When they can do this, they will be able to come up with the answers a lot quicker and easier.

The way you do this is to get your child to pick a spot above eye level on the wall in front of them. They need to stare at it until such time that they can notice the walls around them and pick up things in their peripheral vision. It helps if you put an interesting sticker somewhere on the wall above eye level and use a magician's hat when they are learning. This will make the process more fun and interactive. If you start really early with this, then you will see a new habit form. Outstanding results when learning and recalling already studied material will follow.

Use of Colours

When we are in kindergarten and even primary school, the use of colours is encouraged, and children have a great time learning with them. This seems to cease in the high school years, and learning becomes black and white. Having studied neuro-linguistic programming, it is my duty to let you know that colours help immensely in the learning process. Always encourage your

"Your children will become what you are;
so be what you want them to be"

David Bly

children to use different colour pens and markers, because this will enable them to remember and recall their learning at a faster rate.

Mind Maps

Mind maps are diagrams that represent a certain subject or idea in the centre and have other words, ideas, tasks, and items linked to that subject. They are used to generate, visualise, structure, and classify ideas. They are a fantastic aid to studying and organising information, problem solving, making decisions, and writing. When creating mind maps, the person uses both the right and left cortical skills of the brain, and this aids to improve learning and significantly increase the recall of memory. To learn more about mind maps, I would suggest reading up on the Internet about them (Google 'mind maps') and teach your children how to use them and implement in their studies.

Visual recall

Like expanded awareness, putting the material we are studying in our visual recall area will improve future recall of what was learnt. The visual recall area in a normally organised person is up and to the left. Most people are normally organised. If someone is reverse-organised, visual recall will be up and to the right.

There is an easy way to check where someone's visual recall area is. Ask them a question such as 'What did your room look like when you were a child?' or for children, you could ask, 'What does your favourite toy look like?' These questions will prompt the person to access their visual recall area before they give you the answer. Watch their eye pattern and where their eyes move to as soon as you have asked that question. To be certain of the way someone is organised and their exact position of visual recall, test them by asking at least three questions.

By having the mind maps on the subjects, they are studying around their room just above eye level, children can be taught to place them into their visual recall area when memorising them. This will create a photographic image of the mind map, and it will enable them to remember their study material a lot easier.

Spelling Strategies

Spelling is something a lot of people struggle with. As a child, it may not be a huge issue, but adults can be quite ashamed of this lack of ability to spell. The good news is anyone can learn to be a great speller at any age. Just like anything we do, spelling is a strategy we run. Great spellers are able to picture the words they need to spell out. Poor spellers tend to sound out the words they need to spell and make errors along the way.

Just like in having great learning strategies, the use of colours, and visually recalling, how to spell words will turn you or your child from a poor to a great speller. Here are the steps to follow if you would like to teach yourself or others to become great spellers:

1. Get some flash cards and coloured Texas.
2. Get the person to choose a word they have difficulty spelling.
3. Separate this word into syllables (one syllable per flash card and a different colour for each syllable).
4. Flash the card into the person's visual recall area and then take it down to their kinaesthetic area, which is diagonally opposite to the visual recall (if visual recall is top left for the person, kinaesthetic is bottom right for them) It is very important that they are only taking a picture of the flash card and not playing out the old strategy of sounding it out.
5. As you flash each syllable, get the person to spell the word forward and backwards.
6. Once you go through all the cards, get the person to spell out the whole word.

This exercise should be done a number of times over a period of weeks so that the new strategy gets implemented. It is not necessary to continue doing it long term. When the new strategy is created, the person will know how to take pictures of words visually and subsequently spell them out accurately and with a great feeling that they are correct. The whole idea of taking the flash card from visual to kinaesthetic area is to give the person a good feeling that they are right. Feelings always follow visual and auditory cues.

Being able to pay this forward to many children and adults has been so rewarding and easy. The traditional schooling curriculum does not teach it this way. That is why we end up with so many people being poor spellers. When you have success with helping others learn to spell correctly, get them to pass it on to someone else.

What Children Want

As they grow children, go through different developmental stages. They have needs that vary depending on their age and what is important to them. I would like to share with you each of these stages, so you can build an understanding as to why your child may be acting a certain way.

Within the imprint period of 0-7 years, everything is accepted without opinion, view, or judgement, and there are no ego and filters. During these first seven years, there are different stages:

0-2—is all about the need for *certainty and love*. All your child wants is to feel certain that you will be there, pick them up, and give them all the love they need. Don't deny them this. If they want to be picked up, then pick them up, and they will melt in your hands and stop crying.

2-3—is the time frame where children are all about *power*. Thus, the famously named 'Terrible Two's'. It is at this age that children usually learn how to go to the toilet by themselves and gain a new sense of independence and ability to do things on their own. They like to show you who is the boss, and knowing this should at least comfort you in some way. Your child is not out there to drive you crazy. They are learning to be their own person who can do things for themselves.

3-5—is the age group where it is all about *worth*. Children of this age want to know they matter and the things they share with you are important. It is a time where praise, encouragement, and building self-confidence are crucial.

5-7—is all about *truth*. During this period, children will start asking if Santa is real and want to know the truth about lots of things. Some may start earlier and others much later. It is important we share the truth with our children when they ask. This will build trust and connection between the parent and child.

Following the imprint period of 0-7, there are three further developmental milestones that we go through and those are:

8-15—*Modelling*, which is all about copying how others do what they do because it is appealing to the individual. This may not be considered good or bad by society necessarily.

16-23—*Socialisation* is the need to belong to a particular tribe and be accepted by your peers. This is when children may move out of the home, and social activities have the most meaning to them over anything else.

23-30—*Professional* is when the focus shifts to building a career so that the individual creates security and certainty in their life to start their own family or assure assets for the future.

Knowing about all the above mentioned developmental stages gives you the edge and know-how of your children's needs. It also answers many parents' questions of: 'How long will this last?' or 'Why is my child acting this way?' It certainly has given me peace of mind that everything is OK, and different challenges will follow going forward. Remember it is all part of normal development.

Parents United

There are three keys to raising your children with your partner in peace and harmony. They include:

1. Work hard on your relationship just like you did before children came into the picture. Your partner wants just as much attention now as he/she did when you were alone. Make the effort, plan furiously, and keep the romance, intimacy, and sex going. The closer you are, the easier it will be to make decisions about your children and how you parent them.
2. Decide on what's allowed and what is not acceptable. You want to be congruent with each other and your children so they know that if one person says one thing, the other will be there to back up them no matter what. Giving your children mixed messages confuses them and makes out one parent to be the good cop and the other the bad.

3. Help each other out. In today's society, both parents are generally working out of the home. That's why it is that much more important for both to be working together at home. Coordinate schedules and get more organised. It is crucial to be able to keep up with the demands of children, work, partner, home, and fun. Each person should have certain responsibilities, and as the children grow, they should be given their own to lighten the load and become really efficient at getting the chores done quicker and the fun started sooner.

Top 3 Tasks to Be Completed from This Chapter:

1. Teach your children how to get into expanded awareness to maximum recall of any learning they are doing.
2. Notice what it is you are modelling for your children and start being the example no matter what is going on.
3. Spend an extra four hours with your children per week. Give them your presence.

CHAPTER 11

The Ultimate Secret to Business Success

> Finding your entrepreneurial spirit and making it strong is more important than the idea or business you are developing.
> (Robert Kiyosaki)

You say you want your own business? You are sick of selling your time for money and living the nine-to-five lifestyle. Perhaps you are a stay-at-home parent that is looking for an alternative while raising your children. Where to start? What do you have to know? How can you get the skills needed to be successful in business? And then all the 'What ifs' come to mind . . .

There are only two reasons why people go into business for themselves, and those once again boil down to: time and money. They want the ability to live life on their terms and have the financial security and independence of a lucrative business that can run without them. This is definitely the reason I chose to go into business. Once I had my first child, I realised truly how little time there was left over for myself, partner, and quality family time. Our salaries kept us going, but the time lost being away from each other could never be replaced. This is how my big *why* was born!

The Big Why

The number one reason why you go into business for yourself has to be compelling enough to drive and motivate you towards success. Anything else would be too painful to consider. If you don't know your big *why*, you need to get to know yourself better so you have a clear picture as to why you want a vision of a successful business ahead of you.

The thought of a business never even crossed my mind throughout my twenties. I spent that decade of my life working in the optical industry, where I worked my way up to senior management before I had my son. I knew there was more to life and had read dozens of books on wealth creation and personal development. I did that as a hobby for a very long time. The idea of what I could do did not become apparent to me until some pain was applied to my livelihood and I was pushed into a new direction I am now thankful for.

Driving along a busy main road, becoming a coach was something I had heard of and often thought about. I never researched it or learnt what it involved. My background in psychology and psychophysiology was where my passion for human behaviour began straight after high school. All I knew as I drove on that road was that coaching could be the calling I have been looking for all these years. I discussed it with a few friends and then went to work to find out what it was, how you become a coach, and where can it take you. When I get an idea stuck in my head—everyone has to stay out of my way.

The more I read, researched, and spoke to schools that provided coaching qualifications, the more I loved the idea of becoming a coach. Being able to help others and most importantly myself, first of all, was a great two-for-one package. This business was designed for me! I was so excited, motivated, and eager to begin. My big *why* was the burning desire to have more flexibility, time with my family, and eventually financial independence to spend my time and money whichever way I chose. I no longer wanted to just live within my means. I wanted to expand, grow, contribute, and help others find out the secrets discussed in this book to bring about a better quality of life for themselves and those around them.

Make sure you have your *big why* set in concrete and always in front of you. Mine is on one side of my vision board, and it is constantly reminding me why I put in so much effort, time, and investment in education and marketing to make my business a global success.

Growth Mindset

To be successful in business, a growth mindset is the key ingredient. There are two types of mindsets: growth and fixed. The difference is that one will propel you forward faster than you imagined, and the other will hold you back to a point that you quit and return to the nine-to-five schedule.

People with a fixed mindset:

- think they know it all and are always right
- don't take risks
- remain in the comfort zone
- blame others
- have many reasons/excuses why they are not successful
- disregard education to grow and learn new skills
- surround themselves with others like them
- will quit when the going gets tough

People with a growth mindset:

- learn from others ahead of them in business
- know the importance in investing in education and mentors
- learn from their mistakes and change their actions next time
- take 100 per cent responsibility for themselves and their results
- look for solutions to their challenges
- keep going well after others have quit
- understand the importance of marketing in business and invest in it to create sales and leads
- keep up to date with the latest business tips

Which one of the two do you belong in? It is normal to sway a bit from one to the other due to our need for comfort and security. So long as you spend 80 per cent of your time having a growth mindset, you will experience results that will astound you and those around you.

Reading books on mindset around business and strategies to create the success you dream of is a great starting point to your growth. That is how I began. I spent a decade dabbling in that kind of literature before I made the leap into making it my full-time career. The difference now is that once I read or listen to something, I have the opportunity to test it out in my business and measure the results I get.

Two fantastic resources to get your hands on are: *Think and Grow Rich* by Napoleon Hill and *Simple Strategies for Business Success* by Sharon Pearson. One is a very old but well-known and successful book that delves into the mindsets of super-successful business people and how they did what they did. The other is a book from 2010 that will give you an easy-to-understand snapshot of how business is run nowadays and all the tools and strategies you need to have your own successful business today.

Start reading and having childlike curiosity about business even if you don't know what it is you want to do as yet. One day just before you nod off to sleep, it will come to you. Trust your gut and see it through if it is something you are interested in pursuing. *Working with your passion means you don't have to spend one more hour of your life doing work.*

Credentials

You have your *big why,* and you are getting educated on what it takes to be successful in business. It is now time to work out whether you will need to get formal qualifications for the business you would like to run.

There is nothing more powerful than a piece of paper on your office wall that says you have had the appropriate training in your chosen career to provide professional service to your clients. Qualifications scream credibility, so make sure you are taking the time to get the proper education and then build on it over time to add more tools to your toolbox so you can offer greater value to your clients.

This all fits back into the absolute need for a growth mindset when you set out to succeed in business. When considering how you will obtain your credentials, it is important that you research and ask a variety or training providers what it is you will get out of choosing them for your training. Here is a list of questions to consider asking before making a decision who you will sign up with:

- Are you an accredited training organisation for this field of study?
- What kind of support do you provide your students?
- Is there any face-to-face training, or is it all via correspondence?
- What exactly will I get when I finish my training with you?
- What is your fee structure like?
- Do I have to pay upfront or is there an instalments option?
- Can I have some information sent out that outlines the course in detail?
- Do you have any guarantees with your course?
- What kind of expectations should I have when I graduate via your

institution?
- How are you different from other training institutions, and why should I choose to study with you?

Do your due diligence with a shortlist of different schools, and test them if they run any webinars or free introductory nights you can attend. Sometimes, investment in education can mean parting with a large sum of money. Make an informed decision and stick to it once it is made. It will be clear who you should go with and who is interested to help you succeed.

Modelling Excellence for Fast Results

We have spoken a lot about finding models of excellence for the area that you want to be successful. I am revisiting it again to emphasise the importance of finding individuals in business that you aspire to becoming in your future. Finding these mentors, decoding what they do and how they do it is a fast-track way to the results they are getting. Modelling comes from NLP (neuro-linguistic programming). It works on understanding other people's strategies and thought processes so you can replicate them yourself as a shortcut to outstanding results.

In business, you may want to find a number of mentors that you can model to achieve your goals and vision. Various mentors will have strengths in different aspects of business. Some of the specialty areas can include: marketing, developing business systems, selling, financial intelligence, brand and image, creating successful products, and so on. Choose carefully what will be most important in your business and learn from the experts on how to replicate their skills. Their wisdom won't come for free, so be prepared to invest some money in gathering valuable knowledge. The investments you make today will come back to you ten-fold because of the time you will save doing things the slow way—trial and error.

How to Start a Business

This section alone can be a book by itself. For this reason, I will only touch on a few key aspects when starting a business that are common across most businesses. I suggest that you seek legal and financial advice from experts as to what would be the best set-up for you and your situation. Aside from the

"Many of life's failures are people who did not realize how close they were to success when they gave up."
Thomas A. Edison

experts, there are countless web sites that will explain the process in more depth. Hiring a business coach would also be a great place to start. They will guide and mentor you through the process. Also, they will help you iron out any blockages you may experience through the tough stages in business infancy.

Here are some of the actions and decisions you will have to take and make when going into business:

Business Plan—Before starting out in business, you must put together the all-important business plan. This is not something most people like doing, but going through the exercise will save you lots of time, money, disappointment, or nasty surprises later on. Within a business plan, there are some key factors that must be addressed. Those include:

- Vision statement
- Mission statement
- Business values
- Your ideal client (target market)
- Economic assessment
- Technology items and planning
- Marketing plan
- Location of the business
- Insurance cover
- Web site development
- How much money will you need and loans you may take out
- Various licenses and permits you might need to get

The list could go on and on if I was to be more specific. Find a great business plan template and create your business plan before moving on to the next steps. Have this reviewed by your coach or financial advisor for feedback and a reality check.

Your *business structure* is the first thing that you will need to decide on. There are four types of business structures:
1. Sole Trader
2. Partnership
3. Company
4. Trust

All of the above business structures have their advantages and disadvantages. Most businesses start out as a sole trader/proprietorship and, as they grow, can change to one of the other structures to protect the owner and those involved from being personally liable for debt incurred by the business. Your accountant will be able to advise you on which structure would be best for your type of business.

ABN—stands for Australian Business Number. This is the one thing that every business must have, and if you are from a different country, there would be something comparable you will need to obtain before starting out.

Business name—Even if you are a sole trader, you might like to consider trading under a business name that will form part of your brand, and it may describe also what you do. Business names are also something you must register for a fee, and they must be unique within your country or state.

Business account—Your business account will enable you to be paid and also pay for any expenses incurred within the business. Once you have set this up, you may want to look into getting merchant facilities so that your clients can easily pay with their credit card or even via Ezypay if you end up having the option of direct debit and regular instalments that come out at the same time each month.

Once you have those key areas organised, the next step would be to find the place where you will run your business from and purchase all the essentials you will need to get started.

Budget

A business budget is essential to your success. You must invest money to make money! Some key elements that a business budget should contain include:

1. Initial set up costs (which may be a one-off) and recurring ones
2. Rent or loan repayments
3. Marketing costs and budget
4. Printing and stationary
5. Utilities costs
6. Wages paid out

7. Education expenses
8. Networking
9. Internet marketing and design
10. Travel and catering

You will be able to expand on the above list depending on what kind of business you are going into. In the beginning, you will need to allocate a big proportion of the budget to marketing. This one key area will make or break your business. If you learn to be a great marketer, you will have a very successful business in no time at all. You can have the best product or service in your hands, but if you don't market it effectively and with personality, then it will remain sitting on the shelf. People buy emotions and benefits, not products and features.

Marketing Essentials

The ways you can market yourself and your business are countless. There are hundreds upon thousands of books with marketing ideas. The trick is to find the ones most relevant to your industry and start testing and measuring them.

9 out of 10 Marketing Initiatives Won't Work!

When you find the one that does for you and your business, replicate it time and time again to get the results consistently. The key is to keep trying out different forms of marketing so that you gather enough information and feedback on what works for your business.

Your Brand

Once you have come up with your business name, it is important to design your logo and create the brand for your business. This is something that will be around as long as you are in business. That's why it is important to spend some time and money researching ideas and hiring a professional designer to create it for you. Never share your brand with anyone because it may reflect badly upon you if their reputation is not up to scratch. Treat it with respect and display it consistently across all of your stationary, documentation, web sites, and any other marketing materials.

Just like the McDonald's brand is one of the most recognisable brands in the world, you want to position your brand consistently and over time to achieve a status that in the marketing world is called 'top of mind'. For example, if someone says 'soft drink', what is the first thing that pops into your mind? Most likely, Coke. This is the recognition that you should aim for in your business and niche.

Choosing Your Niche

'The riches are in the niches' say the Americans so famously. The secret to any successful business is the development of a niche within a broader general category. A great niche is one that is an inch wide but a mile deep. What this means is that there is a huge market out there that is after the product or service you are looking to provide but not much competition from other businesses that are doing the same as you.

Select your niche carefully and become the expert in it. Do your research and see what others are doing in the same field as you, and learn how they market to their customers over a period of time. Figure out what is the character your dream client wants you to be, and become that. Spend time learning who your target market would be and what problems keep them awake at night that you can solve via products or services you will provide.

Your Web Site

For most businesses nowadays, their web site is the shopfront window to their business. The face of marketing has completely changed and expanded since the Internet. This has become the first port of call for most people. You don't even have to leave the comfort of your home to have a successful business. Knowing how to market on the Internet is different to traditional marketing and is a special niche in itself.

Make sure you consult with professionals when it comes to your image on the Internet. Your web site look and feel will need to reflect who you are and exactly who your ideal client wants to do business with. Give something away for *free* of huge value in return for people's details. When they see what you give away for *free,* they will wonder what it is you have that can further help them solve their problem. This will help you build your database and create relationships with the leads generated over a long period of time. You do not have to wonder how you will keep this going, since there are many web sites out there that allow you to put together sequences of emails that get generated automatically. You do the work once, and it is actioned time and time again as people join your tribe.

If you are new and starting off in business on a restricted budget, I would like to share with you a couple of web sites where you can outsource work and have it done for a fraction of the price.

Elance—*www.elance.com* is a web site where experts in various fields such as graphic design, copywriting, web site design, editing, illustrations, and many other services bid for your job. You post a job you need completed, enter a price range you are willing to pay, and you end up with proposals from all over the world. You can ask lots of questions, and it is a very secure medium through which business can be conducted quickly and affordably. I have used them many times without any issue, and the quality of work has been outstanding.

Send Pepper—*www.sendpepper.com* is a web site that helps you create your auto-responder emails through which you build relationships with your database. It is easy to use, and there is a low monthly membership fee. The $29-per-month option lets you communicate with up to 2,500 subscribers. The software monitors how many people open your email, manages those that want to opt out, and monitors how many click through on any links you may be sending out. Your web site should be set up to collect details which directly go on to your database list.

Growing Your Web Presence

One of the last key points I would like to share with you is the importance of having a strong web presence. The Internet is a huge place where you can get lost if you don't know what you are doing. Here is a list of the top seven things you can do to increase your web footprint and grow your business exponentially:

1. Have your web site search engine optimised by an expert.
2. Submit articles to free article submission web sites that will generate traffic back to your web site and create backlinks that increase your profile.
3. Create videos and post them on You Tube for traffic redirection to your business web site. Videos are a powerful form of marketing today, and it is helpful to embed them on to your web site so that your customers can see you and get a feel for you.

4. Social Media—Make sure you are a part of this phenomenon where you can also advertise and build relationships and followers for your business. It makes everything more casual but still lets your people know what you do. The three big ones to be a part of are: Facebook, Twitter, and Linkedin.
5. Have a blog and write an entry each week.
6. Work on generating incoming links from other sites. This could work like a joint venture where you link to someone's web site, and in return, they link to yours.
7. Speak at events and invite people to visit your web site to receive something for free that you have specially created for them.

The beginning of every business will pose lots of challenges and unanswered questions. You will play the role of expert, bookkeeper, marketing manager, copywriter, secretary, sales executive, and many more other roles that big companies have assigned to specialists in that field. Being in business is a journey and not a destination. Each step and action that you take will bring you closer to hiring your first employee, each system designed will replace you needing to be there in the long run, and each product you create will remove the need for you to sell your time for money.

Do what needs to be done, get coached on areas you are weak in, and remember to invest in your education.

You Are Either Green and Growing or Ripe and Rotting

Top 3 Tasks to Be Completed from This Chapter:

Even if your goal is not to set up a business today, here are a few tasks you can do without spending any money. It can be a review of the potential something has that you are passionate about, and you will learn a couple of skills around planning and social media.

1. Can you turn your passion into a business? Think about what you love doing, have a lot of experience and knowledge around, and how it may help solve a problem people would pay money to have solved.
2. Create a business plan around it.
3. Get involved with social media even if you are not thinking of starting a business. You never know who you might meet that may present you with an opportunity that's too good to pass by.

Afterword

When I think back on my journey into coaching, weight loss, and change in lifestyle, I realise today the enormity of the potential to grow and discover new ways to reach levels of success that was only in my distant imagination years ago. I know today that in my future, I will be experiencing a different level of success, and I look forward to being on that journey.

The journey contains all the small milestones of wins and some disappointments. Looking back now to just a year ago, I can see the power, action, and impact my goals have had on my success. This book was a decision I made eighty days ago that I broke down into manageable bite-sized chunks and did what I had to do to bring it to reality. I trust it will help add value to your life. If you only take a few key items of learning out of this book, then you will see a change in your behaviour and the results you get.

You are in charge of what happens to you. The responsibility is yours only, and no one can take that away from you. Prove to yourself what's most important to you in life and become successful at it no matter what.

1. Take massive *action*. Without it, there will be no results.
2. Educate yourself and get a *mentor* to help you get there faster.
3. Have behavioural flexibility to change what isn't working.

My company, Ultimate Weight Loss, is invested in helping you solve your weight problem once and for all. My approach is personalised, fun, and gets rid of more than just your weight.

Imagine having a balanced lifestyle that lets you focus on what's most important to you—your family, passion, and relationships. The cherry on top is the ability to fit into that sexy outfit you have dreamt of for years.

Invest in yourself and rediscover your self-worth.

LESS STRESS + MORE LAUGHTER = LONG FULFILLING LIFE

APPENDIX A – Weight Loss Journal

Weight ___	Monday __/__	Tuesday __/__	Wednesday __/__	Thursday __/__	Friday __/__	Saturday __/__	Sunday __/__
			FOOD CONSUMED				
Breakfast							
Snack							
Lunch							
Snack							
Dinner							
Snack							
Total Calories Consumed							
			ACTIVITY				
Activity							
Duration/Distance							
Total Calories Burned							

APPENDIX B – Time Audit Template

TIME	Monday	Tuesday	Wednesday	Thursday	Friday	Saturday	Sunday
6.00							
7.00							
8.00							
9.00							
10.00							
11.00							
12.00							
13.00							
14.00							
15.00							
16.00							
17.00							
18.00							
19.00							
20.00							
21.00							
22.00							
23.00							

APPENDIX C – SMART Goal Setting Tempate

My big picture for this aspect of my life is ….

Specific Goal:	
How the Goal will be Measured:	
Reason why this Goal is important to me:	
Actions required to achieve the Goal:	Time-line for each action item:
Resources required:	

APPENDIX D – Mission De-clutter Schedule

Mission Date Started:

TASK	PERSON RESPONSIBLE	DATE COMPLETED
Kitchen		
Bathrooms		
Wardrobes		
Shed/Garage		
Outside Area		
Shelves and drawers		
Office		
Linen upboard		
Laundry		

Mission Date Completed:

APPENDIX E – Home Budget Template

	JANUARY	FEBRUARY	MARCH	APRIL
INCOME:				
John				
Jane				
Total Income:				
EXPENSES:				
Mortgage				
Child Care				
Home Phone				
Mobile (John)				
Mobile (Jane)	Other Expenses:			
Electricity/Gas	Food			
Home Insurance	Petrol			
Water	Clothing			
Rates	Presents			
Health Insurance	Holidays			
Car Maintenance	Pocket money			
Car Registration	Unexpected			
Car Insurance				

Using the above and adding your own categories for Income and Exoenses will give you a comprehensive Home Budget of all your income and expenditure. Create a spreadsheet in Excel for the whole year. Once you have done this once, you can replicate it each year by adding or removing categories depending on your circumstances. Have fun!

www.ultimateweightloss.com.au

"I must admit, at first I was very hesitant to reveal my thoughts. But after the first 15 minutes of my first session I seem to learn many new things about myself. My coaching experience helped me realize the small the things I needed to be doing to improve my situation. Everybody has something they want to improve on and most of the time the answers are right in front of you. With the amount of motivation and direction I received I quickly realized that anything I wanted was achievable!"

Rahul Patel—Optometrist, Oct 2010

"I have had a fledgling business for many years now, making aromatherapy skincare, the products have been selling in one local shop and to friends and family who love them.

However, the business was going nowhere and needed a real shove to get off the ground. My sessions with Natasa gave me direction, the deadlines set to achieve certain tasks were really useful and worked. I felt I had the support and backup from her to take that extra step with confidence. Nothing Ventured, Nothing Gained.

I have now recruited my sister into the business, we are contacting manufacturing companies, marketing and web designers and I feel certain now that as a result of Natasa's help, this fledgling business is GOING TO FLY!"

Many thanks Natasa

Sophie Seldon Truss—Creator & Owner—
Cleanskins Natural Skincare, Feb 2011

"Thank you for inspiring me back to my true calling. Your sessions gave me the drive and energy I needed to re-focus my efforts to achieving my goals instead of wasting time. I am now employed in the industry I love and am on the way to living the life I want."

Lauren Pinzone—Professional Dancer, Oct 2010

"After rather a gruelling 3 years I found myself struggling to fulfil my dreams and aspirations. In just a few sessions with Natasa, she gave me guidance and the tools I needed to view myself in a different light. Her approach was non judgmental which made me open up and discuss things that had been nurturing in me for ages. She offered alternatives and perspectives that were outside my focus. This made me "THINK" and eventually led to "ACTION". She herself is such an outstanding example of commitment, passion and determination, which not only impressed me but also motivated me to start achieving my goals.

The connection that she established between the two of us made all our sessions very insightful, safe and positive. You can tell that she is committed to what you wish for your life with her coaching sessions. Every session with her helped me gain clarity in my needs and the confidence to move forward. Her energy, insightfulness and warmth made all our sessions a success. She helped me prioritize my actions that resulted in an immediate return. I am grateful to her in many ways and would strongly recommend her to everyone. We all do need help and a push at some point in life, there is no harm in admitting to it and with Natasa I am sure the process will be enjoyable and successful."

Namrata Thakker—Public Relations Executive L'Oreal, Aug 2010

"In April 2010 I made one of the biggest decisions of my life. Moving to Melbourne from Merimbula. I knew there was going to be many difficulties and hurdles I would have to face and overcome. Starting a new job, making and forming new relationships and finding a house to move into are just a few of the difficulties I had to face. However life also decided to throw a few unexpected hurdles at me. The passing of two family members, breaking up of relationships and monetary expenses. These incidents caused me to lose faith in myself and people around me, I had low self esteem, was out of routine and feeling very low.

Fortunately I meet Natasa—a lifestyle coach. To begin with I was unsure about life coaching as I didn't understand the true meaning of a "Life Coach". However I thought I would give it a shot. And thank god I did. Natasa has helped me come a long way from where I was standing 2-3 months ago. I had lost all my self confidence and faith in myself. Plus losing two family members was the hardest thing to deal with.

Natasa you have helped me to look at life in many different perspectives and how to overcome fears and hurdles. After the first few sessions I was able to get myself back into routine and back to achieving my goals—the main one being feeling happy again, getting back into routine and my weight loss goal. I am now going to gym 4 or more times a week, I have a budget set, I am feeling happy and moving on from things in the past and remembering the happy times. Natasa you have given me great advice from either your own or others experiences. You have taught me to set goals but most importantly how to achieve those goals and make them a reality, how to deal with unexpected encounters in life and given me helpful tools to understand myself and others.

I have gone back to being my happy self. I am not 100% but I have learnt that it will take time. The healing process is something that doesn't come instantly. Especially after losing two family members. At one point before I started Life Coaching I couldn't see light at the end of the tunnel. However now the light is brighter than ever! Thank you Natasa for being there to help me get through and overcome the hurdles I had to face and how to deal with hurdles in the future. Also for helping me have a better perspective and understanding of situations in life. I am back to being in routine, I'm moving forward in life, I am choosing to reminisce on the happy moments in life and I'm back to feeling myself again! Without you I don't know where I would be."

Thank you so much,
Saminda Ramsay—Optical Dispenser Aug 2010

www.ingramcontent.com/pod-product-compliance
Lightning Source LLC
Chambersburg PA
CBHW031421290426
44110CB00011B/471